"Why does it matter?

It matters because we live in media, as fish live in water. (Many people are prisoners of the media, many are manipulators, and many want to use them to communicate artistic visions.) But today, at this moment, we can and must design the media, design the molecules of our new water."

Ted Nelson, *Computer Lib/Dream Machines.* Intro. to the 1987 Edition, Tempus Books of Microsoft Press, p. 3.

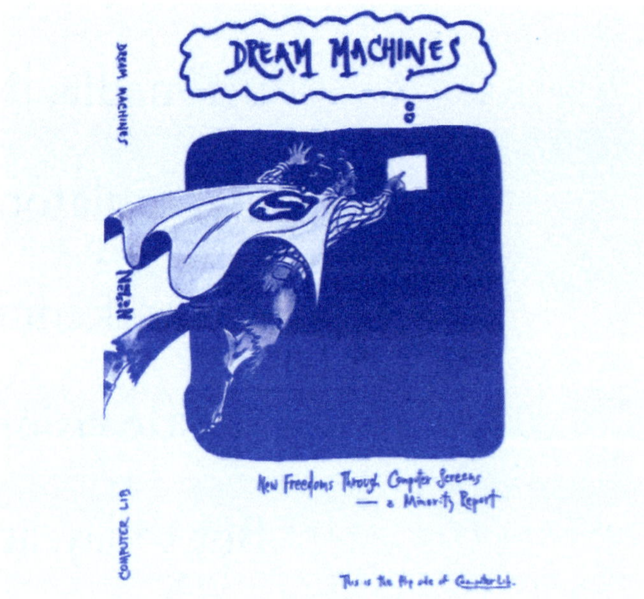

The “Hip Side” of COMPUTER LIB by Ted Nelson, published 1974.

Frieder Nake: The Revolutionary must be like the Fish in Water

A Remark for Jürgen Claus

The morning is cold and it is blue and where I sit, I see a small screen and a larger one just behind, which is better for my eyesight, and then a large window is stretching down from ceiling to the floor. Behind the window, on the other side, the balcony, and I am glad the window is not open, rather closed. But even though it is not open, I feel the cold along my lower leg, it's creeping in wherever it gets through and the old apple tree is hardly moving any of its tiny twigs. It's firmly fixed into the ground, at least that is what they have told me long ago when I was still a kid and did not have a clue of anything.

The morning is cold and also blue as I'm thinking of the fish and dolphins and of whales in the waters that are almost as cold as ice, I guess. But this depends on where you are around the globe. I would not want to be there, certainly not now.

When the American military did not see the Vietcong they decided that they must be hiding under the trees and therefore, in order to see them, got rid of the leaves by applying poison. Successful as this operation was in some way, they still did not see the Vietcong because these clever people had turned the underground into their medium. The revolutionary must be like the fish in water and the American ambassador had to leave the country together with the others who did not belong to it. The revolutionaries had well understood what a medium is.

We do consider elephants and aunts, fish and birds, trees and roses, humans and snakes as things that live. And as I write this sentence, more than ten dozen geese in wonderful formation are crossing the sky above on their path from their sleeping trees to the meadows and ponds where they'll spend the day before, late in the evening, they will return the other way.

Those living creatures need their specific environments to stay alive and feel good. Some need air, and some need water. Ubiquitous and unnoticed. Only when the miracle of the sustaining and embedding substance disappears, do these creatures notice that it's there. The absence of the natural medium is its appearance as a medium.

No technical, no artificial medium will ever be capable of reaching the unnoticed presence of the natural medium. Only in approximation do humans get excited by their artificiality. The ocean is the dolphin's medium. It mediates between its birth and death. Life is nothing but finite and its horizon is called death. The medium of life, however, stretches infinitely. Like the Ocean.

Frieder Nake, 12 February 2019

Prof. Frieder Nake is a Professor of interactive computer graphics at the Department of Computer Science at the University of Bremen, Germany, since 1972. He is a pioneer of Computer Graphics and author of numerous books. His computer artworks are hold among others at the Victoria & Albert Museum, London. Prof. Nake is Editorial Adviser of LEONARDO, Journal of the International Society for the Arts, Sciences and Technology.

Introduction: The Ocean is a Medium

"The wide-open spaces of the sea are a dense network of communications on which the survival of all life depends."

Elisabeth Mann Borgese, *The Drama of the Oceans*

"Medium for me was double-sided, bilateral: natural medium like air, earth, water on the one side – technological medium on the other."

Jürgen Claus, *Salut Au monde!* LEONARDO, 2016

Medium: "a means of effecting or conveying something: such as a substance regarded as the means of transmission of a force or effect."

Merriam Webster

We are children of space. If we experience space, we have points of orientation for our cosmic existence. By understanding space, we understand something essential about ourselves. Both for cosmological science as well as for artistic research, the interface of the cosmic code with the digital code is a productive challenge. If art turns to space, it will do so by using the cosmic code: first detected as a painted code, then emerging as a comprehensive philosophical code and, finally, revealing itself through the digital alphabet, in the last analysis to be the cosmic code. **0**

0 Cf. Jürgen Claus, "The Cosmic and the Digital Code", *LEONARDO*, Vol. 24, No. 2. pp.119-121, 1991.

Elisabeth Mann Borgese, whose work as a sea explorer and sea lover will be discussed later, has dealt with the *Drama of the Oceans* in a captivatingly written book. In the half-century since its publication, the book has lost nothing of its topicality, but also of its deep insight into the context. She imagined the Ocean scientist and researcher as a prototype "of a new interdisciplinary, international scholar, one who bridges the gap between theory and action. [...] conquest of ocean space is not merely a feat in itself, an addition to our treasure of knowledge. It transforms this knowledge. It revolutionizes our concepts of the earth, its genesis, its ecology, its resources, man's role on it, and the requirements of its management and governance." **1**

1 Elisabeth Mann Borgese, *The Drama of the Oceans*. (New York: Harry N. Abrams, 1975) p. 34.

We have to rewrite history one day in the near future, in terms of the *culture of the sea*, as opposed to all the histories which have always been about man on land, about his on–land civilizations and his land-based cultures. **2** For a culturally oriented approach, however, it is extremely important to deviate from this to speak of the special characteristics of river-related, Mediterranean spaces and open oceans with island spaces. The forgotten book of the German Culture Anthropologist Kurt von Boeckmann *Vom Kulturreich des Meeres* postulates in the 1920's the absolute polarity of land and sea. This corresponds to the later "world-historical view" of *Land and Sea* by Carl Schmitt, which in contrast to the first book has remained topical. **3**

2 In this book, the author generally does not distinguish between Ocean and Sea. One should, however, take into account the fact that it is the oceans that occupy 71% of the earth's surface.

3 Cf. Footnote 5.

The book by Kurt von Boeckmann was completed in Munich in autumn 1923. The author was born in Naples in 1885 and died in Munich in 1950. After the First World War, he researched in the spirit of Leo Frobenius the global cultural spaces of the earth and the sea. From 1920 onwards, he was his assistant at the *Research Institute for Cultural Morphology*, now the *Frobenius Institute* in Frankfurt am Main. From 1925 he became known as an employee of Bayerischer Rundfunk, where he served as director from 1927 to 1933. At the 1936 Olympic Winter and Summer Games, he was also active in international radio broadcasting – as director of foreign broadcasts. In his book, he describes the four basic forms that the sea contributes to human activity. **Fig. 1**

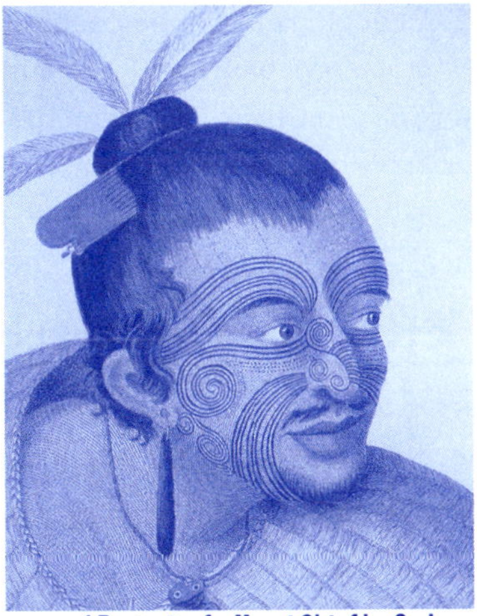

1 Portrait of a Maori Chief by Sydney Parkinson (1745-1771), botanical artist on Captain Cook's first voyage to the South Sea. (Parkinson, Sydney. A journal of a voyage to the South Seas. London: 1784, plate 16.

First: the sea as a source of nourishment. Second: the sea as a means of communication. Third: the sea as a medium of political power. Fourth: the sea as an experience. These four different steps correspond to the economy (1), trade (2), politics (3) and finally art, knowledge, religion (4). In the first three forms, marine activities always remain attached to a terrestrial base. They are mixed forms of terrestrial and marine cultures. A deep gap exists between these and the fourth form of a sea culture. This fourth form is only possible where the powerful influence of the land is diminished to the lowest point, to the status of an island, or a collection of islands, such as the Pacific archipelagoes. Indeed it is in the Pacific islands that we find the origin of the greatest and richest marine cultures of the world. In terms of geohistory, the Pacific cultural space is dominated by the islands, the Mediterranean by the coastlines, the Atlantic by rivers. It is in these terms that a new history might be written – the history of the Planet Ocean.

While the considerations of Oswald Spengler, Leo Frobenius, Kurt von Beckmann, were of a cultural-scientific and cultural-historical nature, the geo-political considerations of the 1920s and 1930s, like those of Karl Haushofer **4**, showed and aimed at an imperialist power-political intervention, one must currently make another rigorous cut in all considerations of land and sea. **5** This incision is due to global climatic change. All considerations about the planet sea get immediate explosive by rising sea levels, melting ice, to the downfall of certain Pacific islands, urban endangerments by water and further disasters. We must approach the seas of the world with imagination and find solutions to immense challenges.

4 Cf. Holger H. Herwig, *The Demon of Geopolitics: How Karl Haushofer "Educated" Hitler and Hess.* (Lanham, MD: Rowman & Littlefield, 2016)

5 I deliberately do not include the considerations of the lawyer and author Carl Schmitt in this context. For two reasons: Schmitt was an active Crown Jurist of German National Socialism and an anti-Semite from the earliest days with full conviction. Second reason: Although Kurt von Boeckmann's essential research had already been printed in 1923, Schmitt did not mention or even admit any reference to the earlier work in his essay *Land und Meer (Land and Sea).* "None of these were Schmitt's ideas. The man read too much." (Thomas Darnstädt, MEPHISTO ALS UNTERTAN, *spiegel special geschichte* 1, 2008) p. 31.

The view of the sea, as Kurt von Boeckmann presented it out of deep knowledge and personal experience, should be a launch pad for us to penetrate the sea with imagination. Influenced by the cultural anthropology of Frobenius, who was eight years older than him, he delivered a building of thought characteristic of the 1920s. In my estimation, no decade of that century was so productive in idea and innovation. The years after the First World War are the *generators* of unique ideas in Central Europe and beyond. We cannot avoid starting with these generators of thought in this book. William Irwin Thompson, with his reflections on the four cultural ecologies, can be counted as a continuation of the cultural morphology of Frobenius and Boeckmann. The *Pacific Shift*, to which Thompson has devoted a thorough analysis in his book of the same name, currently shows itself to be an economic-imperial shift beyond mental and metaphorical shifts, more than Thompson has pronounced, known or perhaps not yet known.

The transition from river ecology to Mediterranean and Atlantic cultural ecology to the Pacific, which he sketched so well, can be felt today in all its economic impact. The Pacific challenge can no longer be grasped by the standards of cultural ecology as he understood it. The Pacific, with countries like China at its borders, is today spilling a gigantic economic wave into both Americas (North and South), Africa and Europe. The sea has become a medium of expanding economic transfers. *Cultural transfers* in the sense from Frobenius to Thompson, on the other hand, are minimized or have disappeared altogether.

The Spanish theatre group *La Fura des Baus* proved that such maritime political events are also mirrored in art and find aesthetic forms with their production of Giacomo Puccini's opera *Turandot*, performed in 2012 at the Bavarian State Opera in Munich. Director Carlos Padrissa staged the basic idea that China in the form of Princess Europe has economically taken over Europe in 2046 and now rules there. "More than 30 years ago, China had rescued Europe from its financial crisis by purchasing its debt, its assets, and its natural resources. China is now the new world power. Turandot, the ice princess, controls as a 'Big Brother' all

Europeans, so that they pay, to the last penny, the debt of the generation of their parents."[6]

6 https://www.lafura.com/obras/turandot/

I would like to conclude this introduction by referring shortly to the term *The Ocean is a Medium*. Question: Does the attribution of the word, as used by Marshall McLuhan at a conference in Vancouver in 1958, help us? Medium here means the environment of services and disservices to him. But the term medium goes much further. The whole title of his book *Understanding Media: The Extensions of Man* creates more clarity through the second part of the title. It is the *extensions* that define the task of the artist. Here McLuhan is a clear-sighted supporter of the artist and his research. "If men were able to be convinced that art is precise advance knowledge of how to cope with the psychic and social consequences of the next technology, would they all become artists? Or would they begin a careful translation of new art forms into social navigation charts? I am curious to know what would happen if art were suddenly seen for what it is, namely, exact information of how to rearrange one's psyche in order to anticipate the next blow from our own extended faculties."[7]

7 Marshall McLuhan, *Understanding Media: The Extensions of Man*. (New York: McGraw-Hill, 1965.) Also: http://web.mit.edu/allanmc/www/mcluhan.mediummessage.pdf, p. 14.

Finally, taking up once more the question and narrowing it. Is the sea a medium for *diving* people? Just as photography or film or video are a medium for me? Once this premise is accepted, the following is striking: Immersed in the primal power of an element such as water, the medium of support or documentation (photography, film, video, etc.) counts for little. How is it supposed to convey temperature, skin contact, the experience of movement? But then vice versa: included in the post-processing system of the video editing station, the medium counts a lot, yes, everything. The fictitious reality of the medium appears authoritarian, at least decisive, decisive. Somehow one is here in the echo chamber of the elements, the elementary, the primary realities – if the relationship is right. Media are mirrors that possess the strange magic of preserving their images, which they take up in the reflection of realities, at least for a while. But then they are also magical stones, they conserve energy and release energy accordingly. They are the carbon pieces of memory. They are fossils, which are actually dead, but from which energy can still be extracted. There they fan out a new reality. And this, in turn, can be processed artistically. So: *Salute to the media!*

I. The Infinite Space of Oceanic Feeling

“To begin to comprehend the mystery of life it is not sufficient to touch and to see – we need to hear, to listen, and thus to unite heart and mind and soul.”

Sir Yehudi Menuhin

This book is about the broad and comprehensive esteem in which we hold the sea, the space of the sea, and thus the unimaginably wide and infinitely diverse birthplace of our ideas of space, economics and philosophy, our knowledge of the planet, its cartographies, its fractally subdivided coastlines and land takeovers, and the many essential aspects of the sea. The fact that we face the sea as an exploiter, hostile to profit, as a great destroyer cannot be concealed. But here my concept of approciation of the planet sea (= *Imagination*) is in the foreground. And a summary and critical examination of my own, sea-related art, which I presented and realized since the end of the 1960s **8**. The book dares to do the balancing act between the past and the present and occasionally invites the present to take on the future. The own past was, as I now find, extraordinarily courageous, occasionally overstated, to give a new life experience by means of *Kunsterfahrung* (art experience) materiality, vividness and conviction. I had many arguments on my side and some arguers against me – I didn’t get to know them all, and that was a good thing. I also had the wind of time, which stood on change and not on perseverance, in the sails I set. This is well expressed in the texts or quotations of the past. In a later picture diary from 1983 I wrote down: “It is the first step that counts”. In the first step, I threw my imagination and ideas far ahead. I had discovered a new planet for myself: the *Planet Ocean* **9**.

8 This book alternates between “the author” and the “I”-form. This results, among other things, from the objective, realized marine and submarine projects of “the author”, which are the experience foil for further developed inclusions. Personal expressions and positions refer occasionally but not strictly to the ego or “I”-form.

9 In 1971 I had suggested a book with this title to the publisher Ernst Bücher of the publishing house DuMont Schauberg, Cologne, which appeared in 1972 (Cf. Books, AV-Material & Institutions for Further Inquiry). At that time *Planet Ocean* was not yet an overconsumed term as it is today.

Much was at the time when I wrote *Planet Meer* in 1971 shifted into expectation, was foreword to future activities. I had little professional diving experience at the time, but the sea was on my side. **10** In a letter to the German writer Heinz Ohff, who was curious and open to my artistic and literary work, I summed up the tenor of the book *Planet Meer*, namely:

10 Diving was at first only the necessary basis to realize my ideas of art under water. In 1974 (till 1979) I took over as editor-in-chief of the diving magazine *submarin - Magazin der Unterwasserwelt* (Munich: Heering Publishing House), which allowed me a professional upgrade with worldwide diving experiences. Cf. http://www.juergenclaus.de/meer.html.

re-invent ART as an opportunity for the EVOLUTION OF MAN. The PLANET SEA, as it was, gives the model case. In a very simplified way, I searched for the EXPANSION OF ART in the new book for an EXPANSION OF MAN. His biological and mental abilities. Discussions with biologists / cybernetics / oceanographers / architects etc. are included in the book. The theme is comprehensively designed (here the preference for Bucky Fuller comes back). But if we do not tackle this PLANET SEA compulsively, but only from the special disciplines, the exploitation effects (large industrial and military), then there is not much chance left for us, but then we are probably moving towards a point where nature, respectively these finely graduated systems in the micro- and macrocosm no longer participate. **11**

11 Letter in original format.

In 1971 I personally met the pioneer of underwater film, the researcher and scientist Hans Hass. The year before he had published his theoretical life's *work* under the title *Energon*, in which 456 pages deal with the hidden common (so the subtitle) **12**. To write the book, he had retired from the underwater world for 10 years, sold his research and film vessel *Xarifa* in 1960 and shot films on land that were widely distributed under the title *Wir Menschen* (We Humans). In our first conversation in Vienna, we began with philosophical-ethnological questions. I was interested in hearing his statements about the artist and the task of fantasy. I included them in my book *Planet Meer*. But a phase of concrete cooperation with him also began.

12 His Energon Theory maintains that evolution can be broken down into three phases: single-cell; multi-cell; and so-called "hyper-cell" organisms. Man, he argued, is a multi-cell organism, but becomes a hyper-cell organism by developing and using technology to enhance his natural physical capacity. In this way, Hass suggested, technology was an evolutionary phenomenon.

Fig. 2

Here is an early example of submarine cooperation between the underwater pioneer and myself. For the Spanish Mediterranean city of Almeria in the early 1970s, a German investor planned not only condominiums but also a hotel with an attached diving school and biological station, as well as

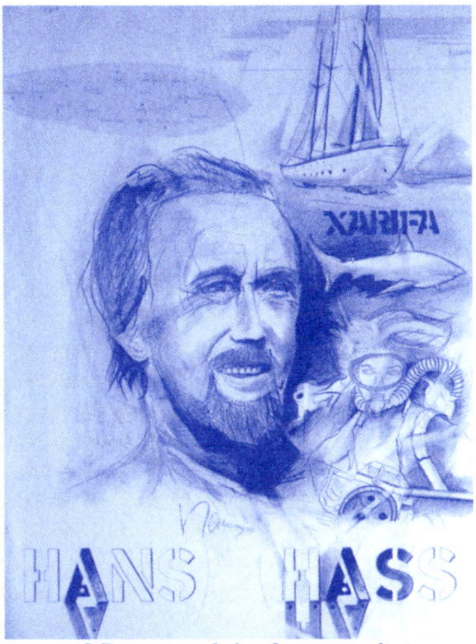

2 Portrait of the Austrian diving pioneer, marine biologist and philosopher Hans Hass, drawn by the author. Above right his research vessel Xarifa; middle right his lifelong diving partner Lotte Hass.

an underwater house. This was designed by the Austrian architect Karl Schwanzer together with his students at the Vienna University of Technology. (Cf. page 49) Hans Hass had pursued and initiated all this with some skepticism regarding the financing. He asked me to build an aesthetic garden next to the biological underwater gardens. This resulted in the *La Parra flower*, which I called it, an artificial sea anemone with about 12 meters long tentacles, made of Lupolen, which was made available to me by BASF in Ludwigshafen. We filled the different colored tentacles with water and anchored them in 12 meters of sea depth off the coast. Ironically, the artistic project was the only one realized, everything else was destroyed, among other things because of the fishermen's lobby, which had presented itself to the government in Madrid because it feared for its fishing grounds. "In the weightless space of the underwater world", Hans Hass wrote in the catalog to my exhibition *World Under Water*, the aesthetic ingenuity of the artist is stimulated. It is no wonder that the imagination is inspired by the very activity of diving since weightlessness underwater conveys a distinct expansion of consciousness to man – experiences which can otherwise only be received in a dream or in the weightless universe in a similar form." **13**

13 Jürgen Claus, *Welt unter Wassser / World under Water.* (Lucerne: Natur-Museum, 1979) p. 1.

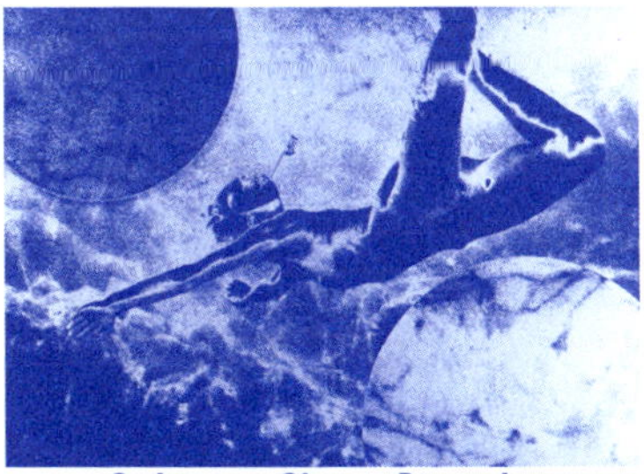

3 Jürgen Claus, *Diver between spheres*, Underwater Photo 1970.

This short remark should be the first indication of how imagination can lead to real objects. And how these objects, in turn, are mirrored and retroactively affect a latently available imagination of the observer or reader. The sea is thus made concrete as a space of experience, learning, knowledge and becomes communicable.

Fig. 3

If this is communicated under the title of an *oceanic feeling*, it must be added that the term stands out from the use that Sigmund Freud, Anton Ehrenzweig and others made of it. How could the term then be understood in the context of my book? I can refer here to the dissertation of the Finnish philosopher Jussi A. Saarinen, which he submitted to the University of Jyväskylä in 2015. It contains *A Conceptual Analysis of the Oceanic Feeling with a Special Note on Painterly Aesthetics.* **14**

14 https://jyx.jyu.fi/bitstream/handle/123456789/45384/1/978-951-39-6078-0_vaitos07032015.pdf

"I maintain that oceanic feelings of self-boundary dissolution are significant shifts in existential feeling. Ordinarily, we experience ourselves as distinct from other people and things, even if there is individual variation in the felt permeability of self-boundaries. In fact, most forms of everyday human interaction require us to experience the boundaries between things, people, and ourselves as relatively fixed and stable. The oceanic feeling is a sudden and often very momentous change in this common existential orientation. Simply put, the felt dissolution of the psychological and sensory boundaries of the self disrupts the taken-for-granted sense of reality and substitutes it temporarily with one that is thoroughly different in kind." **15**

15 l.c. (No page number specified)

In contrast to the physiological, psychological, philosophical definitions, here I propose to take the term literally and not so much metaphorically. It will be connected to the actual experience of the sea and defined by it. In the first chapter, I will therefore turn to the real experience and the poetic, painterly, musical-sounding space of the sea. Here the term very soon becomes more concrete. It is defined and documented by the creativity of the quoted artists. In other words: the experience of oceanic feeling is bound and defined by the resonance space of the arts.

I.1 The Sea as an Object of Poetry

I.1.1 We dive into the Sacred Element: Else Lasker-Schüler

"Born in Elberfeld on the Wupper, in thoughts in heaven, I care for the city of Thebes and am its prince Jussuf. I am neither seventeen nor seventy years old, have no watch and no time. My books run around like this and will one day drown in the sea."

Else Lasker-Schüler

This true expressionist of "all forms present in nature", as her admirer Karl Kraus wrote, has played on the keyboard of all linguistic but also many performative and pictorial forms, has written plays, combative prose such as the "reckoning" with the power of publishers (1925), essays on a great variety of themes and, of course, poems. She called poetry and painting her two companions. The fact that she often, again with Kraus, "leaves no gap between the cosmos and language as a shelter" may also be felt by the reader of her hymnal encounter with the sea. "Her element was the water, not the water of the Tegernsee, but the sea with all that belongs to it: beaches, islands and ships. She has identified herself with water countless times, drawings of ships adorn her letters... 'I am water, therefore I am not a woman', she wrote to Hanns Hirt." **16**

16 Sigrid Bauschinger, *Else Lasker-Schüler. Biographie.* (Göttingen: Wallstein, 2004) p. 252.

In an essay under the title *Das Meer* (*The Sea*), Else Lasker-Schüler (1869–1945) creates in just a little over 40 lines and a subsequent verse of six lines a sea space that is as personally evoked as it is based on mythical sketches. Totally self-explanatory, completely devoted to the experi-

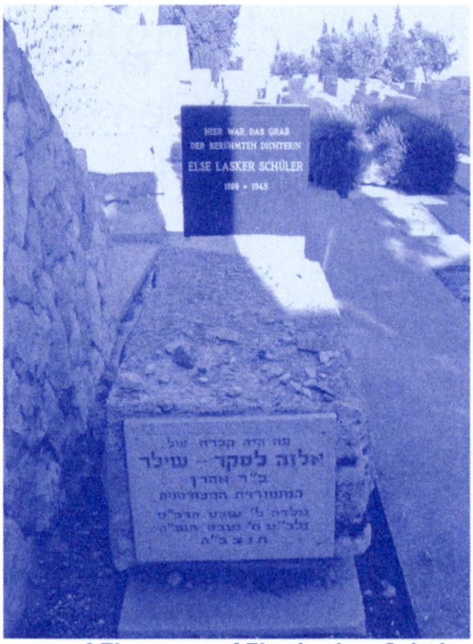

4 The grave of Else Lasker-Schüler in Jerusalem.

ences of her own physicality as well as those of the sea, she breaks any separation between herself and the sea. It is a poem written in prose. Here are the opening and closing passages of the text.

"The sea, too, had once been surrounded by the body before it breezed away. The sea is the wide flowing soul 'left' to the world. The sea is of this world. But the Spirit of God floats over its waters. We dive into the sacred element and deliver ourselves from all earthly heaviness. Ships glide across the ocean from continent to continent. One always wants to embrace and worship the beatific water. [...] As the field bird screams over the grain, again and again, the anxious yellow tone over the trickling dark wheat of the sea. We were staggering with the big water and got into the net of the fog. When it was light, you hurried on into the world; but I stayed on the jetty and refreshed myself with the fresh, refined flower of the green foaming ocean. His water never smells as bitter as it did in the early days of God. Shell and salt and algae and starfish mingle, and the fish gives from the mother-of-pearl of its scales to the must." **17**

17 Else Lasker-Schüler, *Werke und Briefe. Kritische Ausgabe.* Vol 4: *Prosa 1921-1945 Nachgelassene Schriften.* (Frankfurt am Main: Jüdischer Verlag, Suhrkamp, 2001) p.1 96/197. http://www.deutsche-liebeslyrik.de/else_lasker_schuler_seite/lasker_schuler_prosa10.htm

Fig. 4

Else Lasker-Schüler has wrested her poetry from a permanently unruly vita. Poetry is not always created in ivy castles or gardens (Stefan George, Rainer Maria Rilke). The stoniness of her grave carries fate on. "Here *was* the grave of the famous poetess ..." it says on the memorial stone at the Jerusalem Mount of Olives. In this life, there were poetic fixed points that gave orientation to their own personal cosmos. She makes full use of the original German language in her poetry with associations; she seeks and finds union, be it in love, be it with God, the stars or the sea. Her poems are memories in which words rely on their power, on their ability to associate. They form the energetic substance that becomes imagination. From her refuge in Zurich, where they had driven the attacks of the National Socialists, she traveled twice across the Mediterranean to Palestine. Then after her third crossing, she stayed in Jerusalem. She did not return to Zurich, her right of residence had been revoked. The *oceanic feeling* accompanied her until her death in 1945. Coming back to the short and so impressive prose text *Das Meer* by Else Lasker- Schüler, we finish here with an excerpt from the dissertation and later book of the German literary scholar Iris Hermann.

"The sea becomes an allegory not of a context of meaning, but of a place that serves as a mirror and playing surface, a space in which diverse imaginations have their place. The sea is the space for delimitation, dissolution, and dissolution that has been mentioned more than a thousand times. It is the place of the most diffuse, contourless materiality, that which replaces form in the state of losing oneself. It has no physicality, it is the possibility surrounding the body, the infinite space of oceanic feeling. Life here is traced back to its original substance, water, it has reached its starting point and perhaps its end point. In whirls of ecstasy, the ego is drawn down into an unconscious primeval field, the space of above all light-sensible emergence. I figure and sea space merge, then I can no longer be distinguished from its surroundings."[18]

18 Iris Hermann, *Raum-Körper-Schrift: mythopoetische Verfahrensweisen in der Prosa Else Lasker-Schülers.* (Hamburg: Igel Verlag, 2009) p. 60.

I.1.2 And this is a Sea Song like it has never been sung: Saint-John Perse

Alexis Leger (1887–1975), who gave himself the pseudonym Saint-John Perse as a poet, had spent his youth up to the age of twelve on the Antilles island of Guadeloupe – "trees rotted at the bottom of the bays black as wine". From 1914 he was in the diplomatic service, a collaborator of Aristide Briand, was deprived of all offices in 1940 after his decided criticism of the appeasement policy towards the Third Reich. His hymns to the sea, as one might call *Amers (Seamarks)*, appeared in 1957, about the same time as his return from North American exile. Until his death, Saint-John Perse lived mainly on the French peninsula of Giens, surrounded by the Mediterranean Sea. His poems, initially in very small editions, appeared from 1909 onward, for example under the title *Images à Crusoé* (*Pictures for Crusoe*), which had already been determined for Saint-John Perse. The great poems include *Anabase* (1924), *Exil* (1942), *Vents* (1946), and the poetry of *Amers (Seamarks)*, which is particularly noteworthy here. *Seamarks* are regarded as the epic-lyric design of a New World. In a solemn expression reminiscent of hymns, the poet sings of the sea, on whose shores tragedies, princes and lovers step to free man from his torpor, proclaim his true destiny and renew his connection with nature. Even more insistently, however, it may be said in the poet's own language. The summary of the theme of the poem, which he has delivered in the letter to a friend, gives an intensive insight into the whole project. I summarize from it.

"And I chose the symbol of the sea as a mirror of this destiny (add: man), as a place where everything converges and from which everything radiates: a true 'geometric place' and orientation board and at the same time a store of eternal forces from which man, this insatiable wanderer, feeds himself, so that he completes himself and surpasses himself. [...] The sea, our obvious boundary, to which all impatience and all growth aspire, seemed to me, inside the poetry, as the solitary arena and the cultic center, as the 'stage space' or the altar table of the ancient drama, around which the action rolls and before that the figurants and protagonists take up position, each in his human peculiarity nevertheless a representative of the ancient human earth, which has always been at stake."**19**

19 Saint John Perse, *See-Marken.* (Zürich: Coron-Verlag, ca. 1960) p. 313. Translation by the Author.

How do you read the lyrics of Saint-John Perse? Fragmentary or in sections, aleatorically, led by the play of leafing through? Or read them according to their four given parts, systematized, reads them aloud, one even surrenders more to the sound world of associative words than to understanding, is this even communicable? Saint-John Perse writes from lifelong experience, in our case the seas, the coasts, the coastal formations, the coastal cities, the coastal and marine inhabitants. That is one more reason to select this poet with this work as a poetic reference to the sea, to the worldwide ocean. At the speech awarding the Nobel Prize for Literature on 10 December 1960, the Swedish poet and writer Anders Österling compared Perse with Hölderlin and referred to the intellectual range and intensity of his language: "He borrowed metaphors from all fields of knowledge, all epochs, all mythologies, all continents. His great poems are reminiscent of the seashells from which cosmic music is believed to be heard."**20**

20 Saint-John Perse, l.c., p. 21. Translation by the Author.

Seamarks brings the claim of Homeric poetry to the poetry of the middle of the 20th century. Are we willing to take it up? As you may see, I have been fascinated for decades by the rhythm of language, from which I took the titles of several of my own pictures, and have many questions and few answers. I leave myself partially to this language. For its interpretation, I take reinforcement from the indicative (by no means explanatory) texts of Saint-John Perse himself, but also from his companions. Here is another passage from the sea marks:

"[...] sea of Baal, sea of Mammon, sea of every age and every name; o sea of elsewhere and of always, o sea promise of the longest day, and that which surpasses all promise, as the promise of a stranger; innumerable sea of the report, o sea you nameless farsightedness!"

One of the companions of his poetry mentioned above is T. S. Eliot, who was almost the same age as Perse and who, among other things, provided the English edition of *Anabasis* with a precise foreword, which may also be valid for the *Seamarks*. T. S. Eliot answers the above questions about the reading comprehension of Saint-John Perse well and one might almost say "pragmatic" (= instructions for handling). "The reader", says Eliot, "must let the pictures fall into his memory one after the other, without immediately asking for the rational meaning of each one. In this way an overall effect is achieved." **21**

21 T. S. Eliot, „Vorwort zur englischen Ausgabe", in: Saint-John Perse, *Anabasis*. (Munich: Piper, 1961) p. 69. Translation by the Author.

The infinite space of oceanic feeling has long been explored by poets or philosophers and researchers close to poets. This section applies to them. The real energetic symbolism of the sea – vastness, the beach, the blue, the turmoil, waves, marine organisms, fish such as snails and shells – which triggers poetry and can be grasped in real life, found its echo in the works of many modern poets and philosophers. In addition to the poets mentioned above, there are many others that could be quoted. Rafael Alberti as well as Gaston Bachelard, Pablo Neruda, Fernando Pessoa or Gottfried Benn and Bertolt Brecht. It is certainly no coincidence that the seas were one of the ten pillars or landmarks of Hans Magnus Enzensberger's *Museum of Modern Poetry*, published in 1960. In his explanatory statement, he said briefly: "The element appears in it as an object, as a metaphor, as a parable" **22.**

22 Hans Magnus Enzensberger, *Museum der modernen Poesie*. (Frankfurt am Main: Suhrkamp, 1960) p. 19.

I.1.3 Jürgen Claus: Poem to the Sea

1
My sea, my soul
my long-drawn-out dream
my sound
my drums
my dance
my restlessness
my fear

2
We cross the sky
down there
frothing up
the sea

3
It was the clearance
in Okinawa
in the old building
once again the light
in the China Sea
occasionally flying over
coral islands
Night or day
Sea down

4
Nothing replaces
You
ocean
but everything is in you
ocean
Birth Death Dance
where are the dolphins?
The night will teach us
to spell the dream

5
Redfort contains
cool water
in many cannulas
no more

6
Remain only dream
the branches are already blooming
the night is full of light
the day is green
so the sea
down there

7
Goddesses are today
noticeable
the sea gathers up
introduces them
o Goddess o Sea
o Light o Colour

8
The relatives of the seas
islander
The night sends the prince ahead
I don't know where I am picked up
the flights are princes
in pairs
the sea meets
with the night
o dream

9
The surf
the swell
the night
the rhythm
the sexes –
the night throws
over the day
the sea remains
without entourage
heirless
under the evening the night
under the night: humidity. 80%

On board JAL flight from Okinawa
August 2nd, 1975.

"And once I wake up and am the sea."

Rainer-Maria Rilke

The sea – but also the rivers and lakes – have always given the painters the opportunity to apply the liquid painting agents to a liquid element. This applies to East Asian brush painting or European oil painting of the 18th and 19th centuries. Mountains and water are the main motifs in Chinese painting; they stand for the primordial polar principles of yang and yin. Anthropocosmologically speaking, mountains and rocks represent the bone structure of heaven and earth, water the blood, and watercourses their veins. Thousands of pictures, graphics, drawings, photographs, films, and videos would house an image museum of the sea. The flowing, sparkling gives birth to the bodies of the sea, including the shells that convey the sound of the sea and inspire the buildings.

Manuelism in Portugal (Manuel I reigned 1495–1521) brought maritime art and architecture to a climax. All this, however, also against the background of growing sociopolitical tensions that were the downside of global maritime expansion. Manuelinic, in the words of Miguel Esteves Cardoso, was "the boundless, crazy attempt to turn the dominion over water and water – into stone. The water of the sea is the Portuguese medium: the Mare nostrum. This style is not art. It is ambition. Not aesthetics. But politics. No reflex. A projection. In it, one discovers the dreams. They were dreams as big as the world. The anchors, the knots and the algae made of stone, what remained of the dream: lost symbols of an old wish."**23**

23 http://www.s-d-s.de/kirchenbau/html/ornam08.htm (Translation by the author.)

I will try to throw some light on artists who have been required by the sea to performance in an often novel, excited and sometimes erroneous way. Here the sea is captured with its energies, with its colors and its specific light on canvases. The excitement of the sea crystallizes in the painted picture. *Later*, we will be interested in how art today encounters the immense potential of the sea in the form of pictorial field research. This no longer takes place on the painted canvas, intervenes directly in the space of the sea, responds medially in the form of installations, films, photographs.

In painting the sea becomes a monster, in whose depth monsters live. On the other hand, shells and snail shells fulfill the longing for natural beauty. Dutch painting of the 17th century took up these geometricizing housings, placed them in the picture, created an understanding between the observer (the collector) and the variety of forms taken from the sea and washed up on the coasts. The viewer of Caspar David Friedrich's sea paintings looks over the back of a human being onto a distant sea that reveals its force of nature in th e stacked ice floes. In 2007, Anselm Kiefer used the painting *Eismeer* (*Sea of Ice*) from 1823 to 24 (also known as *Die verunglückte Hoffnung*) as the occasion for a sculpture entitled *Verunglückte Hoffnung* (*Crashed Hope*), a maritime dialogue. In Friedrich's work, the ship, created after exactly detailed studies, also has symbolic significance for life in general, for arrival or departure. William Turner, almost the same age as Friedrich, then deconstructs the reality of the sea into a light space that no one dared before (and after him up to Monet). Not the representation, but the surface itself becomes the space of experience for the viewer. More about this below. In 1883 Arnold Böcklin painted women's bodies (nymphs) and centaurs in the *Game of Waves*, who no longer encountered the elemental force of nature in the sea, but who enjoyed the element of water, exploiting it for their own pleasure. About four decades later, Lyonel Feininger crystallized the sea and the sailing ships, which he observed and experienced during long stays on the Baltic coast. Sailboats then appear as motifs to be completed by the viewer in Andy Warhol's *Do it Yourself* (*Sailboats*).

In 1828, at the age of 53, the painter William Turner, on his second trip to Italy, exhibited paintings framed by thick ropes. Is it a demonstration of the scurrility attributed to him, or a reference to something else, such as a counter-attitude to the academic procedure of framing the picture, or a reference to the increasing importance of motifs of the sea and rivers in his pictorial world? (Turner occasionally masqueraded as Admiral Booth.) The sea was a projection surface of a cosmos of light, applied with bright colors, smoothed on, scratched on. Certainly, he also painted its turmoil, the elements whipped up by storms. Often with very precise knowledge of their details, he placed fishing boats and warships in his maritime color contexts. It was the time when the British fleet established and expanded world domination. The existence of the kingdom depended on the protection of its coasts; the sea was everywhere. 1857, only six years after Turner's death, the photographer Gustave le Grey, trained in painting, took up sea themes in his first apparatus pictures, some of which combined two negatives with different exposure times. Let's make a 100-year leap in time to the Japanese, New York-based Hiroshi Sugimoto, eminent photographer of seascapes. He took pictures of the sea for decades and later tilted the large-format pictures by 90°. The originals, the sea, often presented at night and moonlight, evaporate, Sugimoto releases it as a familiar connotation and abstracts it instead in his silver gelatin prints. "In late spring 1982, I saw a beautiful sunset from a cliff in Newfoundland, at the same time the full moon rose in the east. And the way I stood there in the fresh air, I felt like a figure in a painting by Caspar David Friedrich. For the first time in years, I felt like I was leaving my body. I floated high above the earth and looked at the moon above the sea, while another I – a dot – stood spellbound on the ground." **24**

24 Hiroshi Sugimoto, *Revolution*, exhibition catalogue Museum Brandhorst, Munich 2012/13. (Berlin: Hatje-Cantz, 2012. Cited here: Brita Sachs, „Der Wanderer über dem Nebelmeer", *Frankfurter Allgemeine Zeitung*, 19.11.2012.)

"Living phenomena spontaneously generated from water and air in the presence of light, though that could just as easily suggest random coincidence as a Deity. Let's just say that there happened to be a planet with water and air in our solar system, and moreover at precisely the right distance from the sun for the temperatures required to coax forth life. While hardly inconceivable that at least one such planet should exist in the vast reaches of the universe, we search in vain for another similar example. The Mystery of mysteries, water and air are right there before us in the sea. Every time I view the sea, I feel a calming sense of security, as if visiting my ancestral home; I embark on a voyage of seeing." **25**

25 www.sugimotohiroshi.com/seascapes-1

The Nordic obsession of Edvard Munch with the sea is documented in numerous pictures and graphics. He painted and drew back portraits of people who, like a distant echo of Caspar David Friedrich, stand lonely and lost by the sea. In the fable *Alpha and Omega*, which he created during a long hospital stay in Copenhagen, he combines 22 lithographs with a text reminiscent of ancient mythical traditions. Alpha lived with the woman (Omega) on an island where they were the first humans. At the end, Omega was bored, "one night, as the golden column of the moon swayed in the mirror of water, she fled on the back of a deer across the sea, to the light green shores under the moon. Alpha remained alone on the island. One day the children of Omega came to him, a new generation had grown up on the island [...] He despaired. He ran to the beach. Sky and sea were red like blood. He heard screams in the air and held his ears. Earth, sky, and sea swayed, and he felt a deep fear." **26** The world-famous picture *The Scream* (four versions, between 1892 and 1910) implements this dramatic experience. Under the title *Despair*, Munch also thematizes it in the lithograph cycle. Two years or 19 years after van Gogh's death in the later versions, another artist finds cosmic nature in the curvature of the graphic line as the presence of fear, connectedness, embeddedness. In Munch's work, the sea almost always has the character of reflection. This is also the case in his famous murals in the auditorium (Hall of Ceremonies) of the University of Oslo. *Solen* (*Sun*), 1911: A crystallizing sun shines over the sea. The rocky coast is rounded off by the energy of the ray crystal. The painter becomes a light researcher.

26 Edvard Munch, „Alfa og Omega", in: Werner Timm, *Edvard Munch. Graphik.* (Braunschweig: Westermann, 1977) p. 77. Translation by the author.

I.3 Ocean in Concert

"Do you want to see the sound too?"

Johann Gottfried Herder

We have mentioned poetry and the world of the sea painted on canvas with examples from classical modernism. Now, in the third section, we turn to the sound world of the sea, as it was realized by Claude Debussy with his composition *La Mer*. But first Murray Schafer reflects on the fundamental experience of the sound of the sea and water. Later, in the third chapter, we take up the thread again and show how the soundscape of the sea is currently developing as a musical-compository research work.

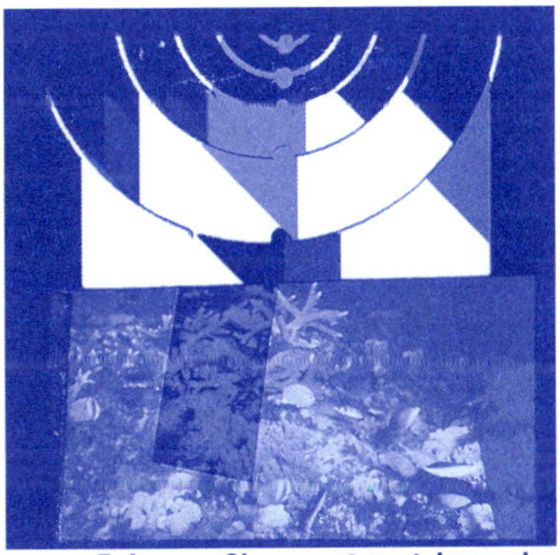

5 Jürgen Claus, a pictorial translation of the sound world under water.

I.3.1 Water as Soundscape

Images and sound pictures: The boy, the girl by the sea, blowing into the mussel, listening to the sound of the sea, early instruments, one can say: mediators between the huge, inconceivable ocean that can only be tamed near the coast and the human being who assigns him languages, sounds, myths. The poetry and images of the sea are joined by music and the cosmos of sound, triggered by or appropriated for the ocean, the lakes, the rivers, the water in all its three manifestations: liquid, frozen as ice or fog. The different cultural circles have developed their music and sound world which generally originates from the sea and the water. But one can also, as it happens in the following, take the ocean itself to the world of sound. This is the first sea-determined sound sphere that later composers follow. **Fig. 5**

"The first sound", says the Canadian sound researcher and composer Murray Schafer, "was created under the caress of water. [...] In the depths of the ocean enormous masses of water pushed past the imaginary ear of the world. [...] Waves were whipped up to surf and clapped down on the rocks as the amphibian escaped from the sea. And if it turns away from the sea, it will never forget its atavistic charm.

The wise man enjoys the water, says Laotse. All human roads lead to water. Water is the original sound sphere" **27**. Schaffer's pioneering book *The Tuning of the World*, which has a lasting effect on younger generations, begins with the sound universe of the sea. Unlike composers who translated the sea and the water into their sound sequences, he aims directly at hearing the sea, the water in its infinitely varied transformations. Everyone and everything that sounds become a sound transmitter. And we as sound recipients must or may sensitize ourselves to all spheres of the naturally given or artificially added sounds. Incidentally, the Canadian sound researcher sees the music or acoustic environment of a society as an indicator of social processes. Schafer uses the example of a beach walk to describe how the acoustic perception of the sound sphere of the sea occurs.

27 R. Murray Schafer, *The Tuning of the World. Klang und Krach. Eine Kulturgeschichte des Hörens.* (Frankfurt/M.: Athenäum, 1988) p. 23 ff.

"One must restrain the mind in order to grasp the million fold transformations of water when it flows on sand or slate, against driftwood or against the dike: every drop a different tone, every wave a different sound from the inexhaustible white noise. Some sounds fade immediately, others stop. In the sea, both merge into an indissoluble unity. The rhythms of the sea are different: infrabiological, because the water changes tonality and timbre faster than the ear's power of resolution can capture the changes; biological, because the waves sound together with the pulsation of heart and lungs, and the tides go day and night; ultrabiological, because the water is of eternal presence. The sea has made music history. In the vast ocean of sounds thousands of years old, in front of the music of the present like islands, the soundscapes, the sound works of contemporary artists." (Cf. p. 76)

I.3.2 Claude Debussy and the Compositional Mathematics of the Sea

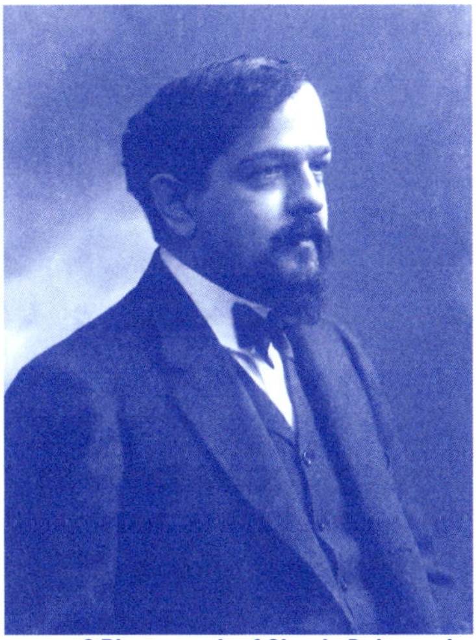

6 **Photograph of Claude Debussy by Paul Nadar in 1908.**

Fig. 6

The German art writer and exhibition curator Günter Metken characterized Claude Debussy (1862–1918) well by seeing in him or in his compositions, apart from the *Préludes*, not the cheerful-sunlike quality of the Mediterranean, but the Atlantic. "His realms are wind, clouds and vibrating air, the Atlantic endless of the ocean, the sea as the scene of a musicality that unfolds, as it were, scenically, which, like Maeterlinck or Kandinsky, ultimately tends towards a theatre of colors and sounds without figures or action".**28** The composition *La Mer* has an explicit context with Turner's pictures, and this because of the cosmic breath that filled his late pictures. Since Turner's name first appeared in 1891, Debussy has seen works by him in Paris and then in London. Begun during a stay in Bilain in Burgundy in 1903, Debussy actually worked out the instrumentation of the composition *La Mer* near the sea in Jersey and Dieppe and completed it in Paris in 1905.

28 Günter Metken, „Debussy und die Künstler des Fin de siècle", in: Karin v. Maur (Hg.), *Vom Klang der Bilder.* (München: Prestel, 1985) p. 337.

Only the randomness of life made me branch off. I've nevertheless preserved a sincere passion for Her. You'll tell me that the ocean doesn't exactly wash the hillsides of Burgundy...! And that this could well turn out like some studio landscape! But I have countless memories: that's better, to my mind than a reality whose charm generally weighs too heavily on one's consciousness.**29**

29 Debussy in a letter to André Messager shortly after having put to paper the first notes of *La Mer*, in September 1903. Cf. Debussy, Claude, Lesure, François; Nichols, Roger, eds. *Debussy Letters.* Roger Nichols (translator). (Cambridge, Mass.: Harvard University Press, 1987).

The three famous phrases bear the headlines *From Dawn to Noon on the Sea*, *Play of the Waves* and *Dialogue between Wind and Sea*. "With *La Mer*," writes his biographer Jean Barraqué, "Debussy has really invented a process of development in which the original notions of exposition and de-

30 Jean Barraqué, *Claude Debussy.* (Reinbeck: *rowohlts monographien*, Vol. 50092, 1964) p. 127

velopment exist incessantly bubbling next to each other, thus somehow driving the work itself without the aid of a binding model." **30** Can one compare Debussy's second movement, the play of the waves while listening, with images from the history of painting? You don't have to. The composer creates here a sound space of an interlocking, overlapping, moving melody, which is close to the turbulling sea of light of the painter Turner in the visual experience. On the other hand: Debussy's *La Mer*, however, works with mathematical calculus. The notation is in itself an astonishing work of art. The reference to sea sounds is very pronounced, do the harps evoke seagull sounds? The *Play of the waves*, the second sentence: themes or motives are taken up and designed by the violins. Violins here evoke the energetic lightness of the waves on which one can ride. Small solos of the harps complete the set. The third movement, the dialogue between wind and sea, timpani and drum create a rumbling sea.

7 The photo shows the Submarine Center project proposed by Jürgen Claus in 1970. Three spheres up to fifty meters in diameter, built as space frameworks covered with plastic skin. The spheres are flooded by water tanks at the lower end for stabilization.

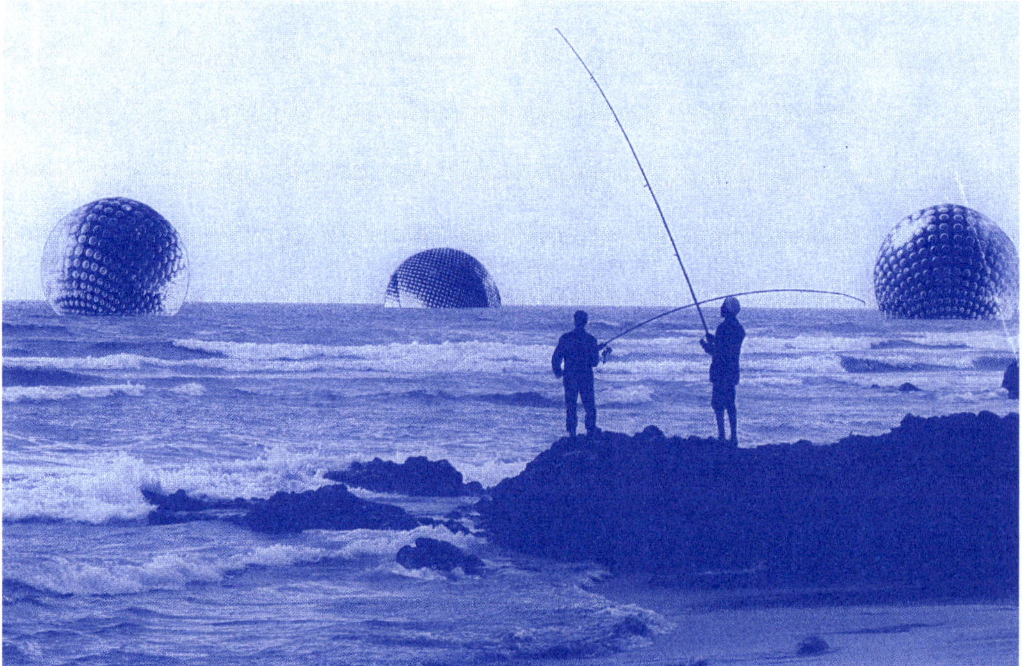

II. Marine and Submarine Architectures

II.1 The Genesis of a Floating Civilization

"The necessity for man to move into the sea, pushed by the biological flood rising within him and the riches contained in the sea, suggests the genesis of a floating civilization."

Paolo Soleri, Architect

Fig. 7

"I don't want to conquer the sea, I want to know its secrets," said Alexander the Great. In the year 325 BCE, his kingdom extended as far as the Indus. He is 31 years old. Near Guadar on the Asian side of the Persian Gulf, he has a kind of submarine built. The material: oak wood, fastened with bronze bands and coated with bitumen. Glass pieces are used for observation under water. The entrance into the diving bell, which is filled with air, happens from below. Together with his friend and fleet leader Nearchos, under the scientific direction of Aristotle, Alexander takes the diving boat to depth. The adventure succeeds – a forerunner of all later underwater voyages. "Under the sea," says Alexander the Great, "things happen that my eyes have seen, without my mind having grasped sense and meaning." Alexander demonstrates with his *Project Depth* that one has to transform oneself into a "fish" in order to observe the fish. The current behavioral scientist, who carries out the observations as field research from his underwater house, does nothing else. One branch of today's underwater architecture is based on this conviction: Laboratories for diving researchers who do not want to undergo the hassle of constant decompression as they emerge from the depths.

Of course, diving into the depths of the sea has also been a commercial enterprise from the very beginning.

Already in Minoan times, in the second millennium BCE, inhabitants of Crete lived from diving for purple snails. The Phoenicians expanded this economic sector. The underwater farm often sketched on the drawing board of marine architects and occasionally perfectly used in science fiction novels, is a logical adaptation to "underwater management". Since the 5th century BCE, divers have also been used for warfare. They saw off stakes, drill – a kind of human torpedo – into the hulls of enemy ships. The Greek historian Thucydides reports about it. Leonardo da Vinci was still wise enough not to publish his methods of prolonged underwater stay, "because of the evil nature of people who would then murder on the seabed". Alone, what did it help! From Wilhelm Bauer, a corporal of the Bavarian Light Cavalry, who built the *Brandtaucher,* the first German submarine around 1850, to the underwater habitats of the 1960s, such as *Conshelf* and *Sealab*, it was the military interest that made money lose. Then Jules Verne's Captain Nemo had a good saying: "The earth doesn't need new continents, it just needs new people". **31**

31 It is the author's frequent mistake to limit the history (here: of diving) to a Euro-centered space. Today we know that around 1400 CE China had the largest fleet in the world, up to 3,500 ships. Some of them were five times larger than those built in Europe, that is, up to 120 meters in length. (For comparison: The *Santa Maria* of Columbus was 19 meters long.) Up to 1,500 sailors had room. There is apparently nothing to be read about divers in the historical reports, but one can assume that the Chinese were also experienced in this art and made use of it.

In the temple of Apollo at Delphi stood the statue of Cyana, the daughter of Scyllias. Both were unsurpassed in their ability to dive and recover the riches of sunken ships. A civilized form of these underwater plunderings appeared as marine archaeology. This has hardly become an issue for architecture yet. However, it is in the nature of things that a carefully conducted exploration of valuable sites can only progress through continuous work by underwater habitats for archaeologists. The decisive impulse for the settlement of the planet sea, however, comes from another side: from the ancient longing for a counterculture on and under the water, which has already led in history to the spectacle of a culture ascended the sea, to the cultural realm of the sea, as Kurt von Boeckmann designed it in his 1924 book. The arc of this counterculture goes over the centuries. From the 17th century, in which John Wilkins, bishop of Chester, foresaw various underwater colonies in which children were born and raised without any knowledge of the country, to Captain Jacques-Yves Cousteau, about whom his colleague Albert Falco noted on the occasion of the *Precontinent I* experiment in 1962: "The Pasha talks like a waterfall – is it wine or pressure? He talks about colonizing the continental shelf. We would all live underwater with women and children. We would have schools and cafes. Almost like in the Wild West." 32

32 Jürgen Claus, „Die Stimme des Meeres. Das Erfolgsgeheimnis von Jacques-Yves Cousteau", *Süddeutsche Zeitung*, No. 130, June 8. / 9. 1985, p.119.

We destroy the seas of the world. One step forward to conservation, improvement is followed by at least two steps backward to further pollution, endangerment, destruction of the seas. Doesn't the settlement of the sea, as it is practiced by architects, bring further burdens, potentiating of the problems? First of all: In view of the chains of oil platforms that burden the coasts and the open sea, in view of the giant tankers and their catastrophes, in view of the momentous mass tourism and its herd camps on the coasts of the world, the number of convinced, militant, practicing marine architects is infinitesimally small. Probably not one of them who is not extremely careful with the fine ecology of the sea.

Something about Jules Verne and his novels about the future of floating islands is still there when we talk about marine architecture today. (Read the next section about Jules Verne's *Self-Propelled Island.*) For most contemporaries, it is something future, nothing concrete, not present. Yet marine architecture has as good a history as land architecture. One only needs to refer to the cultures and civilizations of the Phoenicians, who were largely dependent on mobile, floating structures for everything concerning trade, war, research, and communication. Moreover, shipbuilding is an instructive sideline of marine architecture. For example, in the case of ships, their ability to adapt, their mobility, their multiple mobilities, the way they can obtain energy, their social autonomy over long periods of time. So it is no wonder that Land Architects have repeatedly received inspiration from shipbuilding. One can recall the French architect Le Corbusier, who derived formal and functional inspiration from the ship's structure. At one of his lectures in 1929 in South America, he pronounced it: The steamer "is a big house. There is no confusion here, but the greatest order. Everywhere in the world we have – without exception – a deep admiration for the fast steamer. We are about to rescale the House." 33

33 Le Corbusier, *1929. Feststellungen zu Architektur und Städtebau.* (Berlin: Ullstein, 1964) p. 68. English translation: *Precisions on the Present State of Architecture and City Planning.* (Zürich: Park Books; New edition edition 2016)

II.2 A Self-Propelled Island

125 Years ago. Did Jules Verne Design the Future?

Born in 1828 in Nantes, France, Jules Verne was thirty-four when he had a triumphant success with his first novel Five Weeks in a Balloon. He wrote a total of 98 books. No wonder that this author also dealt with floating architecture. Whereby, as often in his novels, he tells an exciting story with a lot of irony, but in the technical details as well as in prognostics he is very precise. The novel, dedicated to marine architecture, was published under the original title *L'île a Helice* (First published in English in 1896 in a censored Translation as *The Self-Propelled* Island **34**) The following is a brief summary of what is happening on the artificial island and what its technology looks like. At the beginning of the novel, four French musicians are kidnapped in Southern California. They discover that they are on an artificial island shaped like an oval. Their name is Standard Island. The capital is *Milliard City*, which indicates that the millionaires live here. Technically, Standard Island is made of steel plates. The load-bearing capacity of the hull can withstand enormous loads. 270,000 components, each 54 feet high and 32 feet long and wide, are joined together to form a container with a total surface area of 6670 Acres. The floating oval measures 4.349 miles in length, 3.106 miles in width, and when fully loaded it plunges 32.80 feet into the sea and emerges 23 feet out. An outer wall of the island was coated with a novel preparation that prevented any deposition of shells or sea animals. The substructure of the island was filled with earth, which was important for the vegetation. Three-quarters of the soil consisted of lawns with useful plants. The capital *Milliard City* occupied one-fifth of the surface. Its inhabitants had exclusively American citizenship. Those from the north lived on the port side, those from the

34 It was only in 2015 that a first unabdriged English translation by Marie-Thérèse Noiset appeared.

south on the starboard side. The social gradient eventually led to the shipwreck of the island.

The houses on the island were made of lightweight aluminum. Even in heavy seas, the city remained completely calm. Locomotion of the island was not noticeable, the enormous 10 million HP strong screws were hard to be heard in their rotation. The island drifted with 8 knots per hour through a part of the Pacific Ocean between 35 degrees north and 35 degrees south latitude. The route was precisely determined, depending on observations of the island meteorologists. One of the four kidnapped musicians breaks out in admiration of the perfection: “At the end of the 20th century, such islands will be teeming with people. This is how I imagine the comfort of the future.” Already in the 19th century, Jules Verne posed the essential questions concerning maritime architecture: the social status, the form of government of such an artificial island, the management, the building systems, the building materials, the forms of energy, etc.

II.3 We Know Nothing About the Ocean! A Talk with Jean-Michel Cousteau

The author, at that time Editor-in-Chief of the German Diving Magazine *submarin. magazin des meeres*, visited Jean-Michel Cousteau 1976 in Los Angeles on board of the Queen Mary **35**. He talked with him about the profession of an ocean architect. **36** During this time, *submarin* published a report in each issue on selected marine or submarine architects who had intensively studied this question. These include Paul Maymont, Richard Buckminster Fuller, Jacques Rougerie and Kiyonoro Kikutake. Jean-Michel Cousteau, born 1938, is the first son of the famous ocean Hero Jacques-Yves Cousteau and his wife (and partner) Simone Melchior. Besides Lotti Hass, the partner and wife of Hans Hass, she was one of the first scuba divers in the early 1940s. "She was the happiest out of camera range, in the crow's nest of (Cousteau's research ship) *Calypso,* for example, scanning the sea for whales. Nothing would get by her. [...] She lives to spend hour after hour in the wind and the sun, watching, thinking, trying to unravel the mystery of the sea." **37** Simone died in 1990 of cancer.

35 On October 31, 1967, the Queen Mary departed on her final cruise, arriving in Long Beach, California, on December 9, 1967. She has called Southern California her home ever since. The Queen Mary is now a floating Hotel, Attraction and Event & Wedding Venue, home to three world-class restaurants and an icon in Southern California. **36** The text corresponds to the tape recording in archive *project.claus*.

37 Madsen, Axel. *Cousteau: An Unauthorized Biography.* (New York: Beaufort Books. 1986.)

Jean-Michel, already a scuba diver at the age of seven, pursued a degree in architecture from the Paris *School of Architecture* and remains a member of the *Ordre National des Architectes*. Artificial floating islands, schools, and an advanced marine studies center in Marseille, France, are among his projects. But soon he joined his father's *Cousteau Society* for twenty years as vice president. Previously, Jean-Michel Cousteau was President of the *Living Sea Corporation*. The *Living Sea Museum* was built on board the discarded Queen Mary and operated from a house on Santa Monica Boulevard. Various members of the corporation had raised the four million US dollars that the Sea Museum needed to launch. The Captain, as

Jacques-Yves Cousteau was commonly called by all, regarded the sea as the crucible of all life on our planet, the motor of our existence. For him, the sea was the blood of our life and that was the basic idea of the *Living Sea Museum*.

The non-academic nature of the performance on board the Queen Mary made it possible to include invisible but acoustically perceptible messages in the exhibition program. Children were made familiar with the sound world of the sea. The songs of the whales became something natural for them like bird songs or car noise. After financial problems, the museum had to be abandoned. In 1999 Jean-Michel Cousteau, the former architect founded *Ocean Future Society* with Headquarters in Santa Barbara, California. Even many decades after our conversation of 1976, it is revealing to follow on from what has been said. Here are some excerpts of our talk.

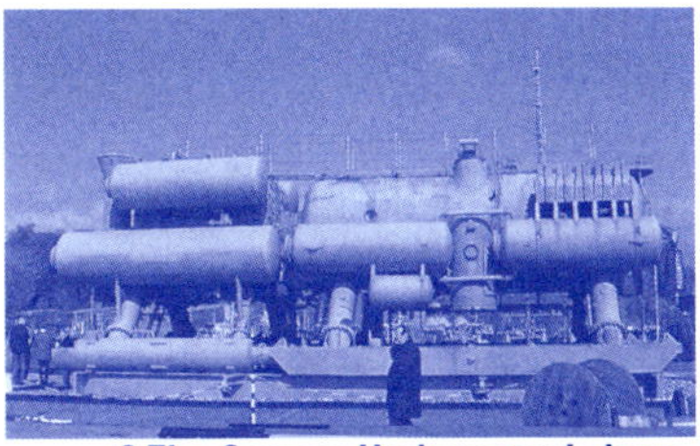

8 The German Underwater Laboratory Helgoland for rough sea conditions. The original habitat was built in 1968/69, the expanded version was used between 1972 and 1981. The Lab is 45,93 feet long, 22,96 feet wide and 22,96 feet high. Divers were able to spend several weeks under water using saturation diving techniques. Today the Lab can be visited at the *Nautineum*, an outpost of the museum in Stralsund, Germany.

"I think we have at this point in history no knowledge at all, there are no specialists of those problems. Nobody has been ever trained about what could be marine architecture. Whether it is floating or underwater. You have some engineers, you have some problems to solve, regardless of the psychological approach, regardless of the costs, because it is an experiment. Regardless of what they create as new problems. There is no one – and I think that is the responsibility of an architect – to be able to supervise from a human standpoint such activity for the good of mankind. I am an architect, even though I am not satisfied with the profession as it is now I still know that I have – if I do some architecture – some responsibility regarding people."

Fig. 8

Floating and underwater architecture, as it has developed since then, will be discussed below. The great upheaval that also took place in this field in the 1960s has continued in different ways ever since. Small and large underwater research habitats have emerged and have brought to light numerous new insights into the underwater world through their observational capabilities for scientists.

"The great opportunity I think is to create that new profession or these new professions – there might be several. You have heard – I am sure – that the ocean is the last frontier.

Well: it is true, we know nothing about the ocean. Since when have we started learning about the ocean? A hundred years? Not even so! Prince Albert of Monaco was named the first real oceanographer in the world. This was 1905 or 1900. When astrology has been learned since centuries and a hundred and thousands of years. Agriculture is known, land architecture: well we have beautiful examples long before Christ. We know nothing about the ocean! Just nothing, we just squash the surface. So there is still a long way to go. Fortunately, many opportunities for young people to enter totally new fields.

There is no language about the ocean. When you say underwater: it is nonsense. Underwater is under the water. So there is a language to be created. There is all new poetry, music, dance – the fact that on land when you dance you fight with gravity, you make tricks to gravity. Underwater you don't deal with gravity. You can be Zero, you can weight Zero underwater. You can play with that third dimension and create three-dimensional ballets. It is an entirely new world, which we not even touched yet. You know that divers, especially deep divers have to use some gas mixture such as helium. Their voice is completely transformed. The stupid approach right now is to try to recreate the original language of that person. So you can understand: if he is an American, you can hear English; if he is a French, you can hear French; if he is German, you can hear German. That's crazy! On the other hand – since you have everybody talking the same way now, when they are underwater – why not create an underwater international language? It's a beautiful opportunity!"

One should not end the reference to Jean-Michel Cousteau without referring to his younger brother Philippe. He worked closely with his father on the famous films of board the Calypso. As an enthusiastic pilot from youth on, he often added aerial photographs to the movies. One of the flying machines, the *Flying Calypso*, became a deadly fate for the experienced pilot. On 28 June 1979, he crashed over the Tejo in Lisbon. His children Alexandra and Philippe JR are now implementing Planet Ocean research into filming and protection of the environment in the third Cousteau generation.

II.4 Kiyonoro Kikutake: Teach us how to Survive!

"Kikutake Kiyonori, teach us how to survive our madness."

Toyo Ito, *Kenchiku Bunka*, October 1975

"But almost nothing has become of my designs for floating projects due to legal barriers."

Kiyonori Kikutake, 2005

The Floating architecture was not a distant utopia in Japan but was started as a necessary consideration to create new housing possibilities for Tokyo, a city of millions expanding at all seams. This can be seen in the context of Kenzo Tange's *A Plan for Tokyo, 1960: Toward a Structural Reorganization*. Tange assumed that post-war Japan was characterized by high mobility and the associated urban infrastructure that had to be specially planned. Kiyonori Kikutake's *Aquapolis* from 1975 for the Okinawa Ocean Expo *The Sea we would like to see* was so far the only real, realized Ocean structure from the circle of the Japanese Metabolists Group. The term *Metabolism* was taken from biology and describes the process of appropriation and release of forces or energies. A common basic design for a new city appeared in 1960 and since then the members have carried out numerous buildings or entire building complexes.

"The capital's population exploded from 3.5 million in 1945 to 9.5 million in 1960. [...] a new generation realizes that a vast reservoir of territory, in fact exists on their own doorsteps: Tokyo Bay, 922 square kilometers of the empty sea right next to Tokyo's intolerably crowded central area of 622 square kilometers. [...] What was previously thought of as an intractable geographical limitation suddenly transforms into the imagination into a new zone for free growth, facilitated by high-tech engineering. [...] The schemes range from wholesale reclamation of Tokyo Bay to islands, floating and semi-floating megastructures, networks of highways and piers for housing, governmental buildings, offices, and industry, stretching 18 kilometers from Koto Ward in the northwest across the entire bay to Kisarazu in the southeast – an entirely new city at sea. The planning of Tokyo Bay is one of several moments in Japan where the phobia of land shortage reaches a frenzy. Tokyo Bay thus becomes a laboratory for artificial ground, which evolves into a core Metabolist concept." **38**

38 Rem Kohlhaas, Hans Ulrich Obrist, loc. cit., p. 267.

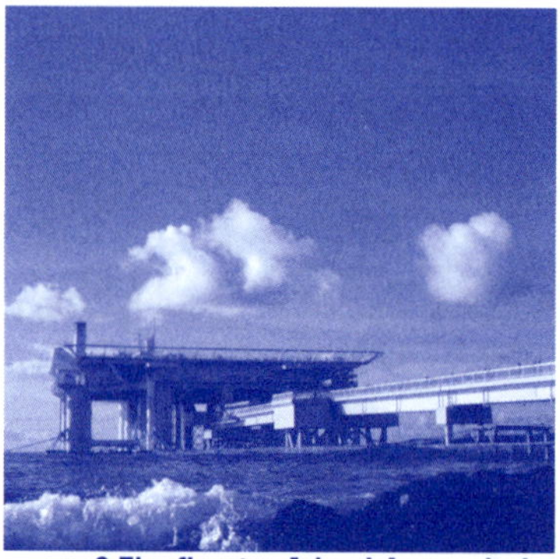

9 The floating Island *Aquapolis* by Japanese architect Kiyonori Kikutake, photographed at the Ocean Exhibition in Okinawa, 1975.

Architect Kenzo Tange, the father figure of the then younger Metabolists, had spoken the word marine architecture as follows. Like urban architecture, marine architecture has two elements: a permanent one and a temporary one. This can be compared to a tree that has a permanent element, the trunk, and a temporal element, the leaves, which fall off and renew themselves. Buildings can grow and die and grow again within the overall structure. The structure remains.

Fig. 9–10

In October 1974 I gave a lecture about the planet sea at *The Asahi Shimbun*, one of the big Japanese daily newspapers. Kiyonori Kikutake speaks as my co-lecturer. It is only a few months before the opening of the first World Exhibition of the Sea on the Japanese island of Okinawa. Kikutake's masterpiece of floating architecture *Aquapolis* is under construction. (The cost of the floating island at that time was about 51 million US dollars.) On four elongated underwater beams stand 16 pillars supporting an upper deck of 108,000 square feet. There are also various lower decks and seawater desalination facilities. Kikutake speaks to hundreds of listeners that marine architecture also needs marine art. I thought of that when I landed on Okinawa in August of next year. Air and sea were equally agitated. Kikutake's seaside town had to cope with a foaming Pacific. But that was planned in. Of course, they knew which unpredictable sea they were getting into.

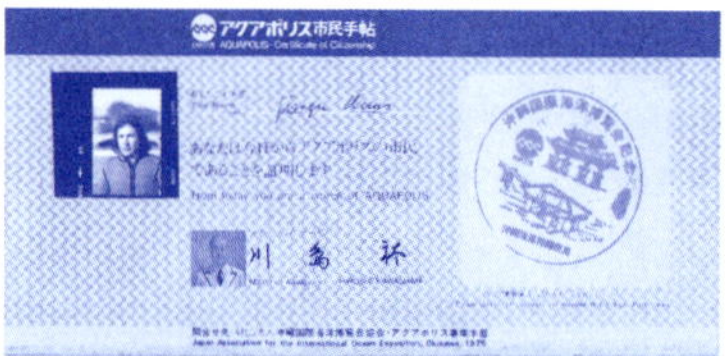

10 The visitors received a Certificate of Citizenship at the entrance to the floating city. This made them citizens of Aquapolis. The document for the author is shown here. Hiroshi Kawashima, the mayor, guaranteed this.

II.5 Is Paul Maymont a Visionary?

The early 1950s are being written. Megastructures line the path of architecture worldwide. Architectures inscribe themselves into the mobile design of urban societies. The city is being rethought and rearranged: politically, structurally, energetically. Architects, artists, sociologists form groups. Everything will be put to the test. The young graduate of the Paris École des Beaux-Arts experiences this new beginning in Japan. There the plan presented by Kenzo Tange for the overbuilding of the Tokyo Bay is hotly discussed. Maymont fits into the discussions about a floating city. The first study of a marine architecture envisages a pyramid-shaped large-scale structure suspended from a supporting mast. A lightweight architecture as it is simultaneously tested and executed in Germany by the ingenious Frei Otto. Square caissons, built in a refit basin or launched as a shipyard, come together to form a city with its navigable canals, water squares, islets, and artificial parks. The construction is protected from the tidal waves by underwater dikes. Each box may contain an autonomous district of 10 to 20.000 inhabitants. A true vertical high-density city (2,500 inhabitants per hectare), it includes on its surface the silent zone of suspended gardens reserved for pedestrians, and below it the multi-level traffic and parking lots. Under the waterline, factories, depots, halls, workshops, and various power plants. Above ground, dwellings, buildings, and villas, offices, public services, religious, cultural, streets on different levels, squares, vertical *metro* constitute a stratified city, with superposed functions.

Eléonore Schöffer, the widow of artist Nikolaus Schöffer, wrote about Paul Maymont's work: "Make no mistake about it, Paul Maymont, one of the 'Visionaries of Architecture' and a fantastic urban planner, remains connected to the most authentic tradition, one that is not made of repetitive conservatism but of attentive listening to a multifaceted and living present. From this knowledge emerge answers in the form of ideas and proposals, but also in the form of advice and the transmission of essential principles and eternal values."**39** Back in France, Maymont can use the experience gained in Japan for a project to expand the maritime city of Monaco to the water surface. I give the floor to Jacques Rougerie, who began his remarkable career as an architect in Paul Maymont's studio at the École nationale supérieure des beaux-arts in Paris.

39 https://www.olats.org/schoffer/archives/maymont1.htm

"This new project entitled 'Thalassa' is shaped as a circular shell. Dwellings and living spaces are organized in terraces around the empty bottom that becomes a water pond with a harbor, beaches, pools, and gardens. The Island would be supported by floating decks in prestressed concrete. The floating rings fixed in the bottom by pretensioned metallic cables constitute 5 levels of parkings, 10.800 mA^{2} of storage, cellar and collective services. 27 radiating mats inclined and hollow containing the elevators fluids are supporting the superiors rings. The first one, at 8 meters above the sea level is interrupted to allow the entrance of boats and hosts stores, warehouses, housings, suspended gardens, restaurants, bars, etc. The second ring consist of seven levels divided into tiers, contains apartments, gardens, terraces, offices, hotels, shops, cultural facilities, games, entertainment. One could imagine that such islands could bring recreation facilities to this new civilization."**40**

40 http://www.jacquesrougeriedatabase.com/Projects/project/4/0

Was Paul Maymont, who died in 2007, a visionary with this and other projects? All too often people are stamped with it who shift their imagination a little further beyond the commercial, established horizons. Whether in his projects *Seismic City* (1959–60), *Floating City* (1960), *Saharan City* (1961) or Polar City (1961), and Star City (1961), Maymont delivers studies where the futuristic dimension is counterbalanced by a solid anchoring in technical reality and by the applied verification of constructive potential. He himself thought that he was an architect of his time. There was a particular vision for him. He tried to solve problems that arose at the time. He did not want to make monuments to their glory.

II.6 Justus Dahinden: The Pragmatism of Vision

Among the buildings of the Swiss architect Justus Dahinden are churches, residential complexes, leisure facilities, but also the unrealized idea of a floating architecture. Early influences on his architecture and thinking include ideas from the Japanese Metabolistic Group and Archigram. All his works are characterized by a strong individual will to form. **41** The same applies to *Athens Seatel*, a plan for a floating hotel in the Sardonic Gulf south of Athens. It is an outwardly shell-shaped floating body which has an inwardly annular amphitheatrical structure. Convertible colored sails on three masts are visible from afar and serve both as a source of shade on hot days and as a visual spatial closure to the rooms below. On the surface of the water, the *Seatel* would be surrounded by a swimming ring, on which a pedestrian would lead footbridge around the floating hotel. Three pontoons leading radially away from the ship are connecting routes to the land and mooring for boats at the same time. The largest diameter of Seatel at sundeck level would be 213 feet. The freeboard height between water level and sun deck would be 50 feet. This floating architecture is functionally divided into four areas: (1) Hotel, catering and events, (2) holidays and entertainment, (3) economy and (4) operation. Four ring-shaped upper floors, terraced against each other, house 155 room units with 310 beds. "Architecture on the water", Dahinden told the author, "is a real way out of the unpleasant situation of conventional urban development. This is being narrowed down more and more by too many fixations. In addition, it is possible to move floating structures in their situation and move them to a new location when needs change."**42**

41 Dahinden wrote with *Urban Structures for the Future* (London, 1972) "the first academic compendium of megastructuralism to appear after the movement had ceased to move" (Reyner Banham, *Megastructure*, p. 201, 202.)

42 Jürgen Claus, «submarin Architektur 1», *submarin. magazin der unterwasserwelt*, (Munich: Heering-Verlag, 5/74) p. 18.

At the end of the short text about Dahinden's sea-oriented designs, a look at another architectural project will be taken. Back in 1973, the *Schwabylon*, designed

43 Cf. the book Justus Dahinden, *Form und Emotion / Form and Emotion*, whose cover is reminiscent of the legendary *Schwabylon*. (Stuttgart: Ernst Krämer, 2014.)

by Dahinden and built in Munich's Schwabing district, was an extraordinarily hip multi-purpose building. **43** *City 2000* contained a cinema, restaurants, solarium, swimming pool and the *Yellow Submarine* (1971–1981). In the form of a thirty-feet-high steel ball, a giant aquarium was installed, in whose 180 000 US gallons of sea water up to 40 sharks and other marine animals cavorted. Dahinden saw in the rising sun on the step pyramid of Schwabylon more than mere original façade graphics. The functional architecture should be alienated and "humanized" through a superordinate artistic intervention. Forty years after its opening, the multimedia experiment had run out in the eyes and accounts of investors and was brutally torn down. "The socio-historical significance is not sufficient to establish a landmark," the city of Munich stated in a comment.

Fig. 11

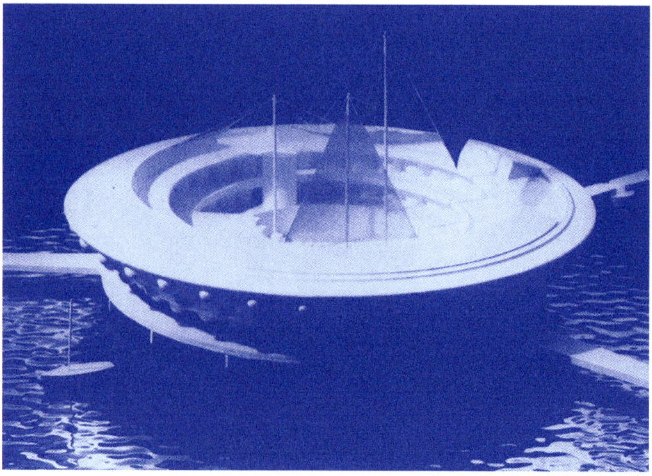

11 Justus Dahinden, *Seatel*, Model of a Floating Hotel.

II.7 Jürgen Claus:

Water as Creative Experience

The author changes at this point from an observer and reporter of marine architectural designs and buildings to his own designs and realizations concerning marine and water architecture. He changes from the neutral form *the author* to the personal form *I*. My interest in "environmental works" in the water and in the ocean started in 1967 by observing how objects in the water change their attitude, their volume, their colors. I began diving, making Underwater photographs of my artworks. I included these works into the concept of *Expansion of Art*. A book with this title (subtitle: *Praxis and Theory of Public Art*) came out in 1970. It has a chapter about *Submarine Structures* – as I called them at that time. A photo of Submarine Structures, 1967, illustrated my intentions, showing free-floating light balls under water. The viewer goes through transparent tubes, which are connected to supply systems.

I described three fields of research for these submarine structures. (1) Water as an energetic fact for submarine structures. Thus ebb and flow and currents can be used as a driving force for artistic forms. (2) A further step is to make such structures visible and experienceable from diving underwater stations or from immersing people. (3) A canon of both static and moving forms and energy events can be set up and systematically explored. Mirrors are conceivable materials that take over reflection and irritation under water. Other materials are light events, rope, and net structures, reflective foils, all kinds of transparent bodies.**44**

44 Most of the submarine structures proposed here from 1967 onward were successfully carried out under water in the course of the following years. More about this elsewhere. (Cf. *Expansion of Art underwater* in chapter three.)

An important further step was my concept of a Submarine *Center* in 1969 with three divisions: an "Experimental Diving Center", a "Center for Theory and Research" and an "Audiovisual Center". I included this concept into my book *Planet Ocean* 1972. In 1970, I proposed an artistic *Exper-*

imental Diving Center to exhibition curator Harald Szeemann for inclusion into his *documenta* 1972. (Not realized.) In different form my projects appeared in the *Aqua-Center* project (with German architect Gerhard Berndt) which was presented at the International Ocean Expo in Okinawa 1975 (Cf. p. 44). From 1978 on a part of the Center was built for the boot-Exhibition in Dusseldorf, Germany. (Diving Center plus exhibition facilities around the Center.)

Fig. 12–14

Jürgen Claus, drafts for an artistic diving sphere project, submitted in 1970 to the curator of *documenta* 1972, Harald Szemann. (Not realized.) Text in the drawing to the right: "The diving sphere is filled up to half with water. From the platform, the divers climb into the water. From here they meet different underwater zones: Light zones. a) A light zone. Spotlights radiate colored light through the water. The divers experience various light zones. b) Here the divers encounter (artistic) underwater structures. c) Sound zone. Here the divers experience the change of the acoustics underwater". Text in the draft on the upper right: "View of the platform at the height of the entrance. The platform is technically a scaffolding construction (*Mero*), which is covered with wooden boards."

Fig. 15–18

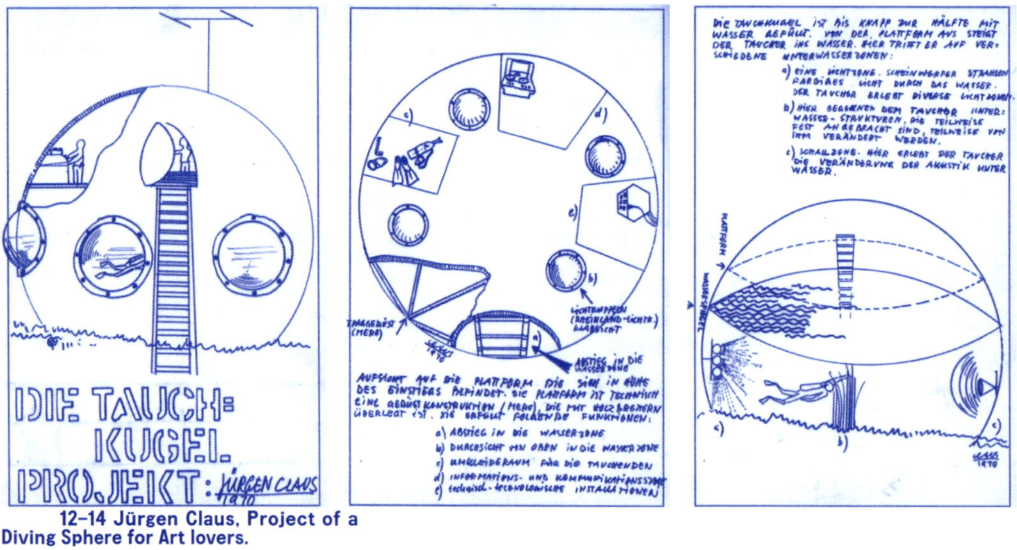

12–14 Jürgen Claus, Project of a Diving Sphere for Art lovers.

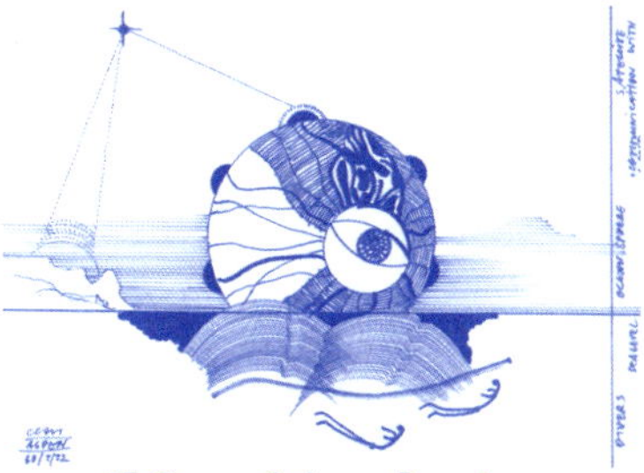

15 *Ocean Sphere*, Drawing on paper, 1972. Satellite communication with a spherical construction on the sea. Divers below.

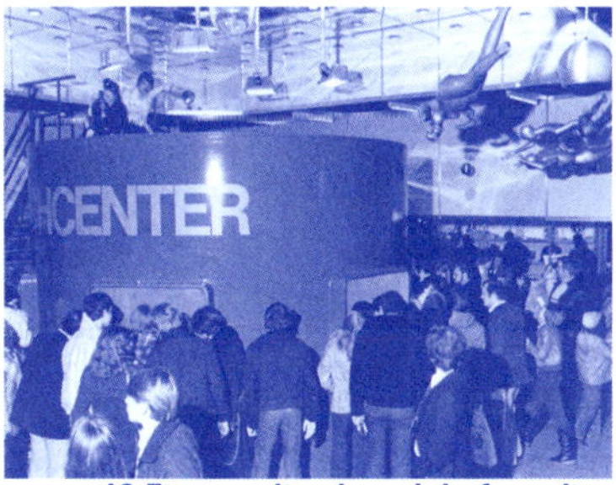

16 First realized model of a cylindrical diving tower for art lovers at the boot exhibition, Düsseldorf 1976.

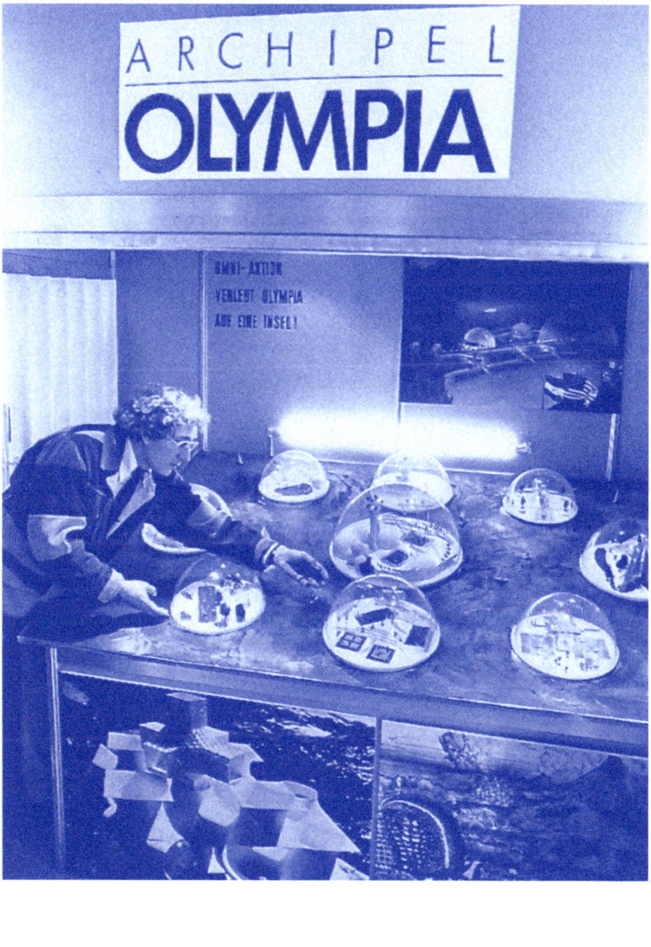

17 Jürgen Claus, *Archipel Olympia*. Presentation of *Floating Olympic Games* with the author.

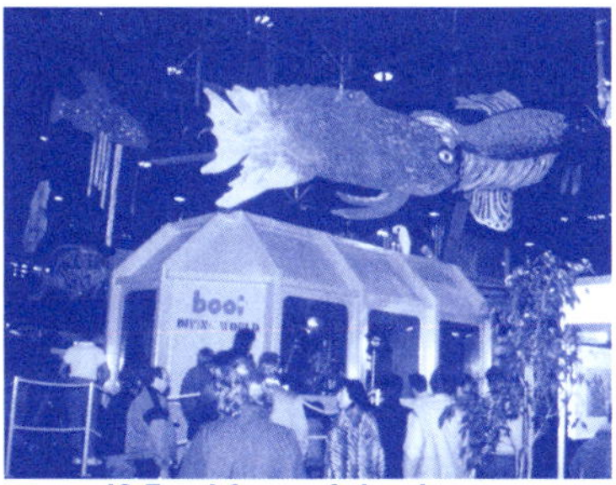

18 Final form of the diving center to the annual boat exhibition, Düsseldorf. Artistically designed surroundings by Jürgen and Nora Claus.

II.8 Underwater Parks and Architectures

At this point, we will visit some observatories of tourist interest, some of which are located in sheltered seabeds. Undoubtedly, they help to intensify the experience of submarine environments. A realistic and concrete impulse to protect marine zones resulted from the idea of national parks. The first suggestions go back to the 1st World Conference on National Parks, which was held in Seattle in 1962. It was recognized that marine fauna and flora, as well as land vegetation were subject to the dangers of destruction. All governments of countries bordering the sea were asked at the time to examine the possibilities for marine parks or marine reserves. In 1964, Dr. Tuyosi Tamira, then President of the *Japanese Nature Conservation Society*, took the initiative in Japan. Two years later, possibilities for these parks were explored in the Pacific countries.

In 1965 the Marine Parks Center was founded in Japan. Eight areas on the Japanese coasts were declared part of the National Park Program. The oldest underwater park in Japan is three hours by train from Osaka. It is located at the southern end of the Kai Peninsula. The warm Kuroshio current comes close to the land. Average water temperatures are 57° and 71°. The first underwater observation tower has been standing here since the beginning of the1970's. It can be seen from far away from the coast through the striking double-cross shape with round windows in a bright red color. A narrow long bridge connects the tower with the coast. The total height of the system is 82 feet, the diameter at the lower end is 32 feet. Later the Underwater Observatory Marine Park in the Red Sea near Eilat became world-famous among tourists. About 330 feet from the coast, the observatory is built around a stair tower. The large observation room is 20 feet below the water surface and allows a view of coral reefs and about 800 species of fish, mollusks, turtles. The

Oceanarium is a huge simulator. In a spacious hall containing 140 seats, a film is screened on three huge high-quality HD screens, and the visitor takes part in a journey through the depths of the Sea. Another variant of an underwater observatory extends 33 feet deep into the clear waters of the Milford Sound, an inlet of the Tasman Sea in New Zealand. The Queenstown Underwater Observatory, located at the Main Town Pier, provides insights into the living world and tells the Maori mythological story of Lake Wakatipu. The architecturally ambitious designs of underwater observatories by Jacques Rougerie and his team are presented later in our book (Cf. p. 54–56).

Among the possible visits to a protected underwater world are the actual dives in zones offered by national parks. One section of the US National Park Service is the *Submerged Resources Center.* Its mission is to support projects for superintendents and partners responsible for the stewardship of submerged resources and to enhance and facilitate public appreciation, access, understanding, and preservation of these resources. On the website of the *National Park Service,* **45** you can find excellent scientific documentation about the Channel Islands National Park, Point Reyes National Seashore, and Micronesia.

45 https://www.nps.gov/orgs/1635/pdf.htm

Fig. 19

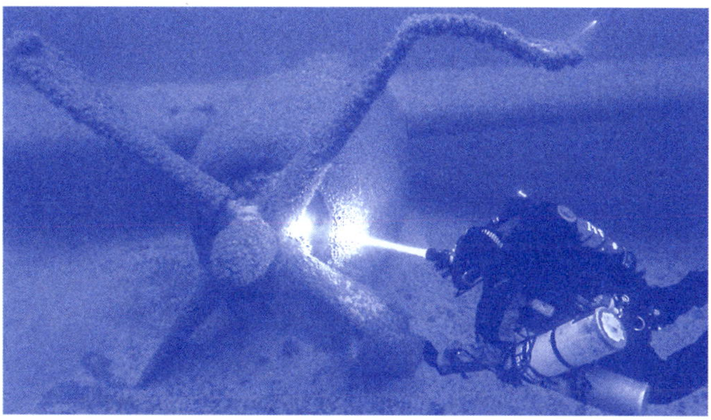

19 Divers of the US National Park Service *Submerged Resources Center* on an underwater archaeological research mission.

II.9 Jacques Rougerie: Inhabit the Sea

"Je pousse mes concepts architecturaux le plus loin possible pour progressivement donner corps et réalité à mes rêves."

Jacques Rougerie

With the architect Jacques Rougerie, we enter the realm of inspired and at the same time realistic sea architecture. Jacques Rougerie spent the first eleven years of his life in Côte d'Ivoire. He got influenced by a friend of his father's: Théodore Monod, a botanist, zoologist, geologist, archaeologist, and geographer.

Monod participated at the invitation of Auguste Piccard in the test dives of the bathyscaphe FNRS II between 1948 and 1954, from which he draws the story Bathyfolages, deep dives, 1948–1954. **46** Rougerie sees the film *Le Monde du silence* by Louis Malle, reads the books by Jules Verne, Arthur Clarke, Isaac Asimov and looks for his own way to turn the enthusiasm of the sea into a profession. From 1964 to 1973 he studied at the l'École nationale supérieure des beaux-arts in Paris in the studio of Auguste Perret and met Paul Maymont. From 1970, his passions for the planet sea and for architecture merged. He founded with his first wife Edith the architecture company *Jacques Rougerie Architectes Associés* in 1972 and teaches at several architecture schools. In 1971, he started with the project of a sea city for Indonesia, planned from local building materials like bamboo.

46 Cf. Théodore Monod, *Bathyfolages. Plongées Profondes.* (La Croix du Sud, 1954.)

In 1971, he started with the project of a seaside village Thalassopolis for the Indonesian Banda Sea, planned from local building materials like bamboo. On the base of the Kai Islands, in a lagoon-like situation with shallow water depth, a warm average temperature of 80ºF and a biologically rich environment, he planned a settlement on the water for initially 1000 people. Rougerie had been studying the local conditions and his proposals were ecologically, sociologically and materially adapted to them. Talassopolis 1 should be based on controlled aquaculture for crustaceans and mussel. The project (unrealized) was followed successively by designs for a floating farm (1973), an underwater village-like complex, a cultural sea center, a floating pavilion for the Bay of San Francisco, an Archeoscope (1976–78), which aimed to open up new working conditions for underwater archaeology.

In 1977 Rougerie was finally able to immerse his first *Galathee* underwater house in the Mediterranean Sea. The unusual, flattened spherical structure was not a bizarre design idea but followed years of intensive study of the micro-bodies floating in the sea and other organisms. *Galathee 1* was designed as an underwater house, which should be mobile, that is to say, could go to various depths up to 50 yards. The large viewing areas are designed to address the psychology of people living and researching in the sea. The task was: research in the fields of marine biology to underwater archaeology. *Galathee 1* could accommodate a maximum of five divers at the same time. The diameter of the steel body was about 6 by 6 yards, with airbags at the edges for stabilization, lift, and down force. *Galathee* 2 followed in 1981, improved a lot, but following the same principle. Mobility was written in capital letters, easy navigation in depth, large observation windows. Divers can stay three times longer in the improved model than in Galathee 1. “Nevertheless”, the friend and architect told me, “Galathee is only a stone of the building for me, is part of a whole underwater civilization whose birth we are experiencing today”. Another sea construction by Rougerie followed: the Aquascope. It is a viewing tower and observation boat, 7,10 yards long, 4.4 yards wide and 3,3 yards high. A corrosion-resistant aluminum alloy supports the two laterally projecting floats, which provide stability. With a 25 hp marine engine, the Aquascope reaches speeds of up to 7 knots.

An Iconic Ship

„Je ne suis pas un Marin, je ne suis pas tout à fait un Terrien, je suis un Merien.“

Jacques Rougerie

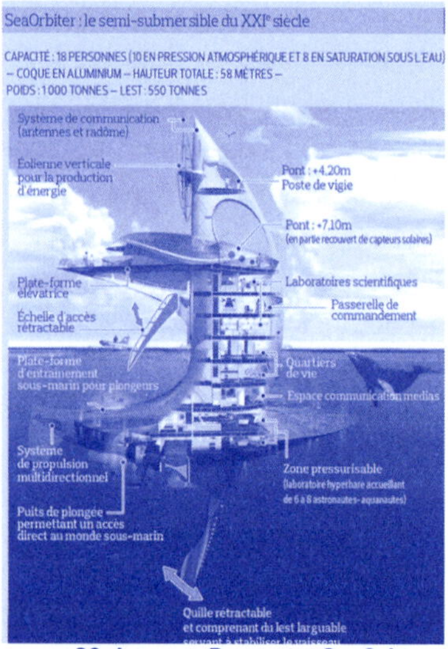

20 Jacques Rougerie, *SeaOrbiter*, an oceangoing research vessel.

SeaOrbiter, 170ft tall, is probably the keenest and most advanced architectural projects of the Paris based Rougerie. It is a spaceship of the Oceans, an aircraft, a flagship, a marine and submarine vessel, a construction on and in the sea like it's never been seen before. The construction began in 2014. Will it be accomplished?

In any case, I believe that this large-scale project not only enriches but also determines the history of the imagination directed towards the oceans. And I will take the liberty of telling you at this point how, from what deep, almost genetic power, the imagination here turns to the sea. I can call Jacques a friend. In my book *SonnenMeer* (*SunOcean*) I have recorded moments of our friendship. I called it an *energy field of friendship.* Here are some excerpts from the book.

Fig. 20

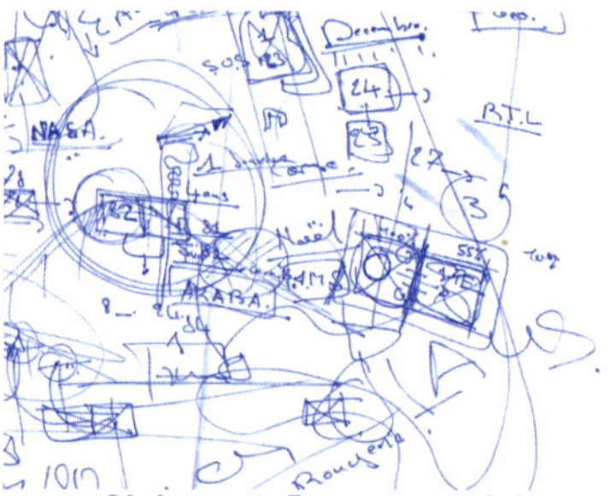

21 Jacques Rougerie and Jürgen Claus discuss developments in submarine architecture in a restaurant in Paris on 7 July 1980. Rougerie captures what is said in picture icons and pictograms on restaurant table paper.

"There's the energy system of friendship. Friendship emerges from a reference system that can hardly be reconstructed later. An example: During a meal together in the mid-1970s in a Paris restaurant, two people, the marine architect Jacques Rougerie and I, meet like clusters of energy. Joint designs and strategies for the future are grouped according to hardly identifiable models. For both of us, the sea is a field of current and future artistic and architectural experiences and concepts. A "genetic" impulse sets forces in motion, supports the planned. Energy quanta are converted into language and will. I remember after decades the energy of concentric circles that animated me in the hours that followed. In the hotel I drew the night through, our conversations encouraged me to go on, much skepticism towards others." **47**

47 Jürgen Claus, *SonnenMeer*. (Cologne: Wienand, 1995.) 14.

Fig. 21–22

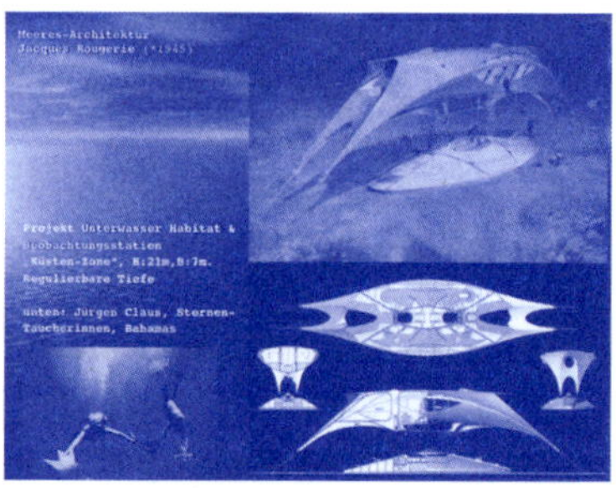

22 A page from the Powerpoint presentation by Jürgen Claus on submarine art and architecture. On the right side the model of an underwater observation station of adjustable depth by Jacques Rougerie. Below left: *Star Divers*, an art performance by Jürgen Claus in the Bahamas waters at Long Island.

II.10 Trans-Architectures for Trans-Societies

In their computer images, marine architects are currently designing a wide range of *transarchitectures*. This term couples architectural forms with the broad notion of constantly changing parameters. Here, non-euclidean spatial designs are combined with musical and algorithmic programs. Distorted, broken, bent rods in space open up an infinity of space. This opens up the no longer manageable, no longer calculable deep space. There, large forms like a sphere of spatially tilted rectangles, grids, rods, which lead to a fluid overall appearance. On the one hand, the origin from familiar polygons is included, on the other hand, the digital hybrid design leads into a nearly cosmic constellation, which distracts the picture far from an architectural concretion. "The computer screen," says transarchitect Marcos Novak, "can be seen as a two dimensional prototype of a space whose dimensions are limited but whose functions change according to necessity and desire. This space, once limited to the user interfaces of our computers, has now outgrown the monitor and has entered the three-dimensional world as a whole." **48**

48 In: Michael Benedikt (ed.), ***Cyberspace: First Steps***. (Cambridge, MA: MIT Press, 1991), 229.

Just as one received a new passport as a citizen of the sea at the entrance to *Aquapolis*, the *Seasteading Institute*, founded in 2008 in California on the Pacific, is also working on models of marine communities that have detached themselves from the land in the communal understanding. In the third chapter of our book, we take up these further questions. At this point, a final word should conclude the subject area of current marine architectures. It must be said that contemporary marine architectures have to live with the fact that on the one hand, everything has become possible in visual computer calculation, but that the real execution has moved far away. To put it even more directly: the algorithm has no practical test aside. For this reason, I hesitate to integrate these calculation constructs into the context of my book. Anyone who is willing to look at the visualization potential of today's software out of curiosity or for playful reasons may do so. If this reminds you of Jules Verne, you should be aware that Verne was also a socially and politically thinking and writing author. However, this is missing from the algorithms.

Fig. 23

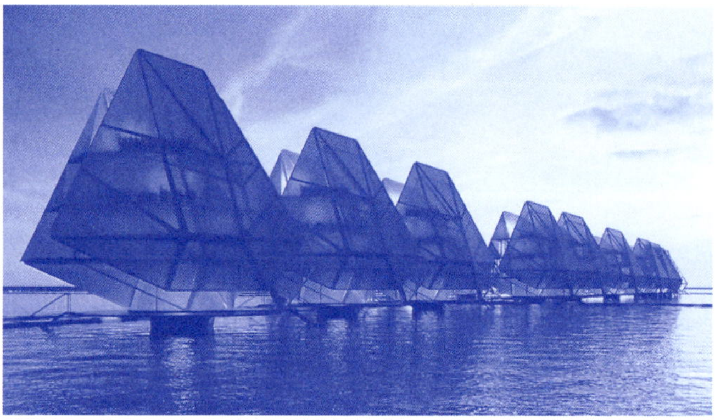

23 The Jacques Rougerie Foundation in France announced 2017 the winners of their Grand Prix. Filipino architect Alam Deo Alrashid (picture), along with Andrew Galano, and Pierre Michael Monjardin, won the *Innovation and Architecture for the Sea award* for their design.

III. Explorations by Imaginations

III.1 Ocean and Space

"Change comes when people care, and there are no better messengers to communicate the beauty and fragility of the ocean than divers who have a direct, emotional connection to the ocean."

Dr. Sylvia Earle, Submarine Researcher, Biologist

"To climb the highest peaks [...] celestial space, to turn our searchlights upon domains of eternal darkness, that is what makes life worth living."

Dr. Auguste Piccard

It is about a century ago that man looked for deeper observation on Planet Earth. He turned to the depth of the Oceans. 1927/1928 the American researcher William Beebe considered various plans for deep-sea cylinders since there was nothing in his opinion like a ball for even distribution of pressure. The idea of a perfectly round chamber took form and grew. By 1929 a steel sphere had been developed and in 1934 Beebe gave the first eyewitness accounts from the deep sea. The history of the diving boats continues with

Trieste bathyscaphe descending in 1960 to 35,814 feet, *Archimède* two years later reaching 31,360 feet, *Deepsea Challenger* 2012, 35,755 feet. On June 27, 2012, the Chinese research submersible *Jiaolong* with two oceanauts reached a depth of 7,062 meters (23,169 feet) in the Mariana Trench in the western Pacific Ocean. **49**

49 Cf. https://en.wikipedia.org/wiki/Jiaolong_(submersible)

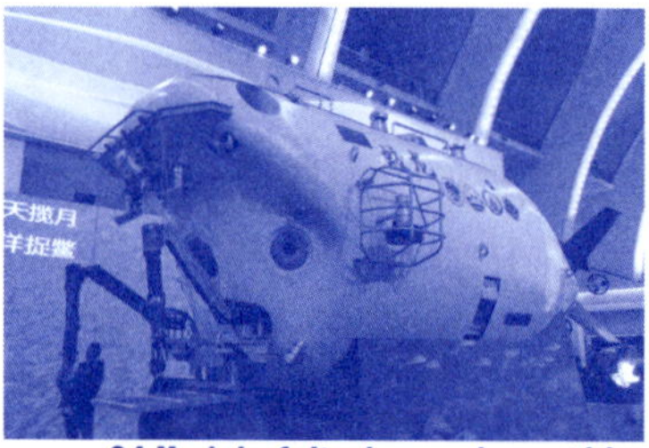

24 Model *of Jiaolong* submersible.

Now we are 100 years further in comparison to the early expeditions of the pioneer Beebe. Each new expedition can build on the results of the previous ones. Yet our knowledge of the depths of the oceans is extremely imperfect. Victor Vescovo, the founder of the US private equity firm *Equity Holding*, has now set himself the goal of exploring the deepest points of the five oceans with a specially built diving boat. Our depth of ignorance about the oceans is quite dramatic. Four of the oceans have never even had a human being go to their bottom. In fact, we don't even know with great certainty where the bottom of the four is. **50**

50 Cf. Rupert Neate, "Wall Street trader reaches bottom of Atlantic in bid to conquer five oceans", *The Guardian*, Dec 22, 2018.

Fig. 24–25

With his $48 Millions expensive research diving vessel *Triton*, Vescovo reached a depth of 27,480 feet below the surface in the waters of the Puerto Rico Trench in 2018. For the first time, a person reached the greatest depth in the Atlantic Ocean. **51**

51 The only other submarine that has explored depths below 22,966 feet (7,000 meters) and is still operational is the Chinese Jiaolong submarine. Cf. https://en.wikipedia.org/wiki/Jiaolong_(submersible)

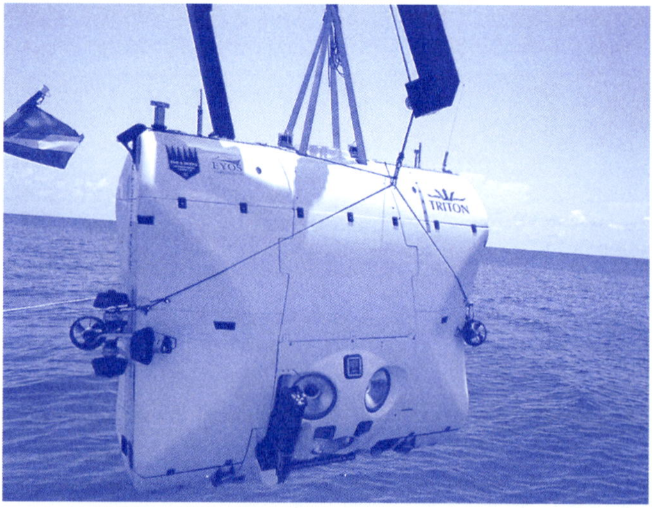

25 *Triton Submarine*, a research vessel financed and developed by Victor Vescovo.

III.1.1 Man in Space and Man in Ocean: a Manifeste

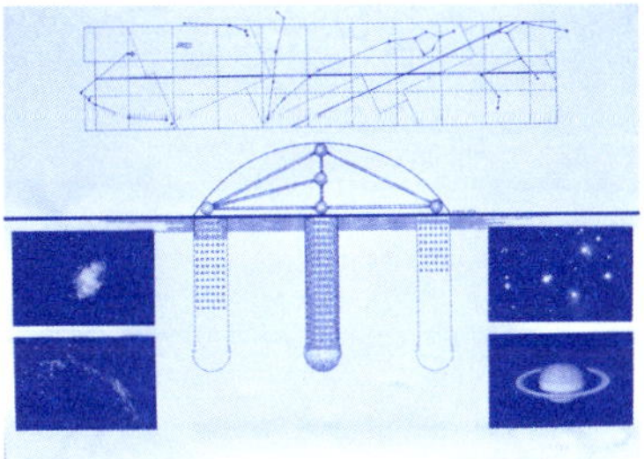

26 Jürgen Claus, Drawing of a *Cosmic Ocean Architecture.* The architecture, resting on large underwater supports, is placed in context with events of the cosmos, here with the star constellation of Aries.

Fig. 26

"From the depths of the sea, I greet my friends of outer space. Both the inner and outer spaces of the Earth reflect our present experiences. These two spaces free us from our everyday burdens. They make us mentally and physically free. The inner and outer space have changed our visual conception of this planet and the entire planetary system. This metamorphosis takes place in us – in the depth of our psyche and in our new knowledge. Such personalities as Auguste Piccard have opened up new territory for us by exploring the sky and the sea. We artists merge the scientific exploration of sky and ocean with human experience. We artists have developed the material for visual adventures in both spaces – namely light, inflatable objects, weightlessness and freedom of movement, the integration of nature and its artistic potential. For the concluding *Sky Art Conference* in 1984, I hope to realize an interplay between man in space and man in the ocean. I will work towards it. (On board Lufthansa flight 793 on 27 August 1981)" **52**

52 First published in the catalogue *SKY ART Conference '81*, Massachusetts Institute of Technology, Center for Advanced Visual Studies, 1981, p. 50. In original German language again published in the catalogue of the third *SKY ART Conference '83*. (Munich: BMW, 1983) 59.

That was the author's message, then at the best active and vital age of 46, to the upcoming first *Sky Art Conference*, which took place from 25 to 29 September 1981 at MIT in Cambridge. Within the group of artists and researchers who turned to space above us, the author belonged to another species who placed the space inside, into the sea. Otto Piene, MIT artist and organizer of the *Sky Art Conferences*, was also an excellent contact when it came to transforming the energies of the sea into a spatial-aesthetic experience. What mattered to him was to intensify the human experience in dealing with the sea so that it becomes an aesthetic experience, and that meant for him a *life experience*. Piene put this into concrete terms in a conversation with the author. “It is not enough for a man to come to terms with technology and become receptive to nature. Everything only makes sense if it combines the great forces of human experience with the elements, i.e. with nature and technology, which has almost become an autonomous element.” **53**

53 Jürgen Claus, *Planet Meer. Kunst & Umweltforschung Unterwasser*. (Cologne: DuMont, 1972.) 61.

III.2 The architect as Disc Jockey: "Bring Something Incomprehensible into the World!"

Gilles Deleuze, *A Thousand Plateaus: Capitalism and Schizophrenia*

Vincent Callebaut

Going to Vincent Callebaut's website is like browsing through a very colorful children's book. There is a 'groundscraper', the opposite of a skyscraper. The bioclimatic tent-like building is (virtually) situated in a field with the most beautiful flowers, lots of poppies. Callebaut designed it as a project for Morocco. All is virtual, everything is a visual offer, all ist pleasure. Men dressed in traditional Thawb strolling.

Furthermore: *Elasticity*, an underwater city where 50,000 people live happily. No wonder that the young architect with these computer images won a first prize in the Godecharle's competition 2001 in Brussels. "Between the gravity of the earth and the weightlessness of water, *Elasticity* is a town without a location. Its organic design gives it birth, life, and death through the assimilation of the submarine universe. It is utopian and therefore does not claim to be transplantation of terrestrial life." **54** Callebaut paints *Elasticity* in contrasting colors of cobalt blue and signal red, distorted perspectives and text insertions, an intriguing world, seductive to the eye that liberates itself from the constraints of a real sea and real architecture.

54 http://vincent.callebaut.org/object/011201_elasticity/elasticity/projects/user

"A recycled interface: the shaped roof, made of 1 km^2 metallic net and wrapped in a coating of expanded polypropylene, is stretched just above the water. It makes a transition of the body's two movements in space: walking and swimming. Its lower curve is the substratum of minerals and trace elements that are indispensable for the formation of new inverted soil, the niche of aquatic plant life. Two parallel glass blocks fix a point on the horizon and reduce it to infinity. The place seems empty, with no space! These two glass monoliths recycle the salt water; one purifies the sodium and the chlorine, the other is kept for fresh water. A bubble of air sucks in the oxygen supplied by the photosynthesis of the phosphorescent algae. The air contaminated by CO2 ejected by the human body is purified. On the one hand, this aquaculture generates the energy for food, which attracts aquatic animal life, and on the other hand, it generates the mechanical and electrical energy of Elasticity. This oceanic beacon compressed between the two blocks of glass is a giant float from which hangs a vertical town, ensuring that it moves according to the ocean tides." **55**

55 Ibid.

For this architect, there is no reasonable reason not to be unreasonable. Callebaut rides his calculating machines like a jockey rides his horses, to madness, to victory. Maybe that's why he puts himself in the position of a jockey, a Disc Jockey. "The architect becomes a true Disc Jockey of the planetary information building the space by mixing and reducing the practices coming from everywhere else outside the field of architecture." **56** Callebaut has read his Giles Deleuze. It gives him a pleasure to transfer his computer constructs to human, so-called human, physical existence. Architecture, he transforms Deleuze's dictum about writing, has nothing to do with meaning. It has to do with cartography, including the mapping of the future, not yet known, countries. Are these computer-ascending cities on the sea, like water lilies, even drawn by us? Do they not draw themselves, *cyborgs of our imagination*? The criterion is the infinite imagination. And it becomes the medium of the untenable, the never possible, that breaks into our dreariness and shames us. The medium, double meaning sense of the word, is named by Philippe Steels from the Belgian pixelab. **57**

56 Ibid.

57 Cf. http://www.pixelab.be

The author avoids becoming a universal critic of these gigantic and super-gigantic Imaginations computations. Why would he? His own biography is marked by visionary maritime brands, only that it was the pencil used at the time, the *Rapidograph* **58**, that depiled, and not the calculating machine. The fantasy has a reality of its own kind. As long as and insofar as it is predisposed, as Callebaut does, to designate a different, positive, ecological world, it is not shameful to turn to it.

58 The leading market position of the manufacturer *Rotring* has led to ink pens being colloquially called *Rotring pen* in the US/English-speaking world.

Fig. 27

Criticism included at all times, but please that kind of criticism that contains the humor, the irony, the human misconception. If you have leafed through the fairy tale books of future floating giant cities long enough, you will be loudly brought to the raison d'être by the present. That means: As the futurologist Robert Jungk proposed and realized with his future plans for workshops *(Zukunftswerkstätten)*: first of all allow the unrestricted imagination to come to words and images. Then the discussion about it openly led. Then the points of criticism are put forward and evaluated. But the criticism shouldn't already smash the approach of a vision, an utopia.

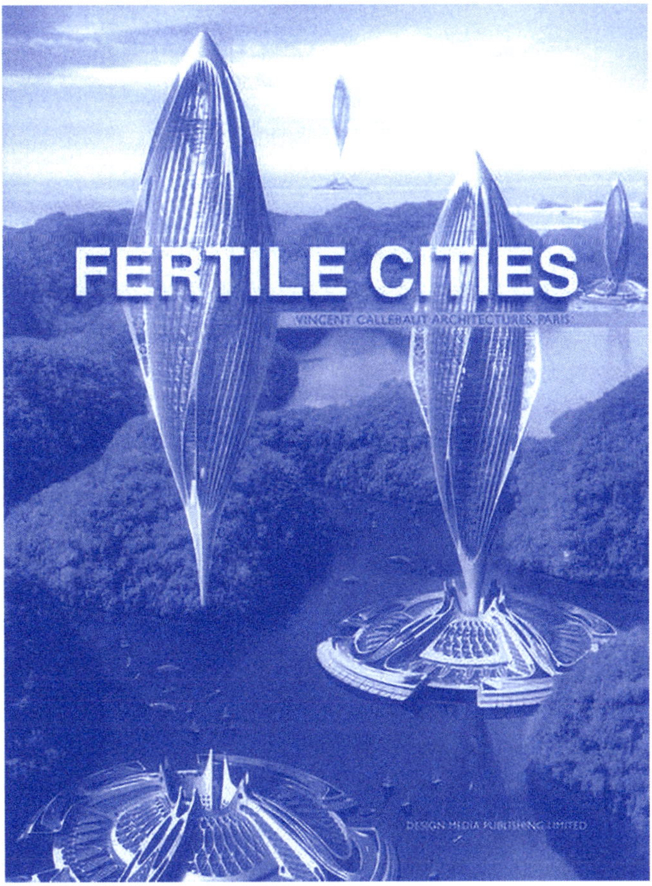

27 Vincent Callebaut, Book Cover *Fertile Cities.*

III.3 The Olympic Games on the Ocean: A Pragmatic Vision

The question, as the author saw it, was: will we have to end the Olympic Summer Games in near future because the organization regarding costs, environmental problems, land and water(front) prizes, etc. will be against the majority of the people? Concerning the costs here are some estimated costs of past Olympic Games. Sydney 2000: US$ 4.7 billion; Athens 2004: €9 billion; Beijing 2008: US$42 billion; London 2012: US$11 billion; Rio de Janeiro 2016: US$15 billion. Greece's billions in Olympics debt led to bankrupt the country for years. *The Olympic Agenda 2020* includes recommendations for developing a sustainability strategy and different transparency measures. Among the many proposals are those of Andrew Zimbalist, a professor of economics of Smith College, Northampton USA. He supports the idea of getting rid of the bidding system and pick a permanent host.

The further the 1960s progressed, the more novel structures became apparent in the field of marine architecture. There were three interwoven questions, which I will briefly discuss here. (1) First, there is the question of the *social status* of floating architecture. This includes questions of communication within and outside the zones lying on the sea. We must also ask about the optimal housing density and political status. Do floating architectures still fall within the competence of the area off whose coast they are located? (2) The second fundamental question raised by marine architecture is about the actual *architectural systems* that can be used for such a floating architecture. The question is about the support systems, whereby column-like structures, similar to those used in drilling platforms, are possible as semi-submersibles, which in turn are flooded in the water. Purely floating structures are also conceivable, with building materials ranging from steel to inflatable tires in a wide range. (3) Finally, a third question needs to be asked: Which *forms of energy* do we work with within a floating architecture? My own answer was already in the late 1960s: Let's use here the renewable energies of wind and sun, possibly tides. Solar technologies are just as suitable for floating architecture as wind-powered technologies. Not only rotors, propellers, etc. should be considered, but also the shape of the sails should be revived, which is an architectural and creative enrichment of marine architecture.

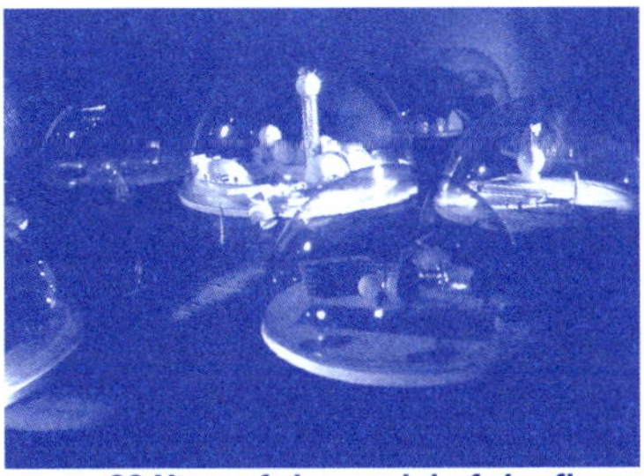

28 View of the model of the floating sea Olympics, designed by Jürgen Claus.

Fig. 28

[Short digression about marine wind energy]

Here is some further information on the use of wind energy as it is presented today also for an innovative marine architecture. Wind power was once a geopolitical force of the first order. Those who caught the winds in their sail corvettes, aligned them and used them for fast maritime traffic, had a head start. In the face of climate problems, start-up companies around the world are currently tapping the potential of wind power at hitherto unimaginable heights. Regenerative energies are intended to regenerate our climate. And engineers are thinking of using natural forces even more innovative. Ingenious: that means inventiveness and cleverness in one. In 2008 *Time Magazine* included a strange flying, energy generating thing, an intermediate form of helicopter and kite, among the 50 top inventions. The Californian start-up company *Sky Windpower* had introduced this flying windmill, more precisely a flying electric generator (FEG). What is driving engineers around the world upwards? Predominantly, but not exclusively, young US American companies are currently dividing the market, but before that the research, the experiments among themselves: *Makani Power*, *Sky Windpower*, *Windlift*. They appeared together at the Airborne Wind Energy conferences held in 2010, starting that year at Stanford University, California.

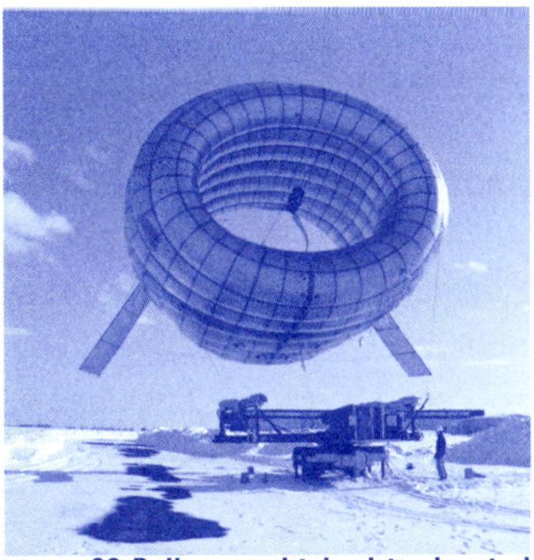

29 Balloon as high-altitude wind turbine.

Fig. 29

High-altitude wind turbines are based on some basic atmospheric factors and use them to develop their projects, all of which are currently being tested. The starting point is the fact that wind energy can be found to a large extent in the higher layers of the so-called troposphere, the lowest floor of the atmosphere, 5 miles at the poles and 11,2 miles at the equator. At a height of 262 feet one can expect an average speed of 15 f/s for the common wind turbines. Multi-

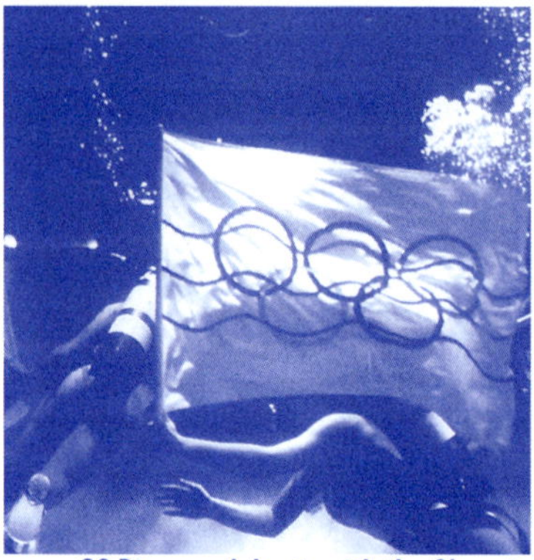

30 Divers celebrate with the Olympic flag the presentation of Olympic Games on the sea.

plying the height by 10, at 262 feet altitude with a wind speed of 23,6 f/s a wind energy harvest of 205 watts per 10 square feet can be achieved. So why not work on using the high-altitude wind for maritime power generation? The worldwide capacities for high-altitude wind turbines have been calculated and published. A scientific network has been established between atmosphere researchers, energy and materials engineers, urbanists and landscape planners. In the future, it will become clear where these innovative energy suppliers and storage media will be tested and finally installed.

[End of digression]

Back to the project of an alternative form of summer Olympic Games on the sea. (Cf. Fig. 28) For an underlying material structure, there are systems in place that respect the natural environment of the sea and are not incriminating. The systems are feasible. Nothing would stand in the way of a Sea Olympics technically, i.e. from the carrier structures and the energy systems. Anyone who does not like such a demand could at least accept it as an innovative game of thought. The basic structure that I have proposed since 1973 is based on nine floating islands. In concrete terms: around the Olympic Stadium in the center – where the traditional major events such as athletics, football, and horse riding take place – there are eight other islands that carry two Olympic villages, the administration center and the press and communication center. Furthermore, each island is dedicated to the swimming stadium, the cycling area, the training camp and a sports facility, which includes various disciplines such as fencing, wrestling, boxing or team sports such as basketball, volleyball, handball, and hockey or new sports included in the Olympic program. An echo of my ideas to relocate Olympic summer games at sea landed by the Dutch architect Koen Olthuis. **59**

Fig. 30

59 „Rio de Janeiro would be able to make world history as the location for the first floating Olympic Games. A strange idea? Not for people who dare to think outside the box. It is up to the climate change generation now." Ken Olthuis, David Keuning, Float! (Amsterdam: Frame, 2010.)

III.4 Evolutionary Architecture. Yona Friedman meets Wolf Hilbertz

"In this beautiful, broken world of collapsing ecosystems, failed states and toxic lies, we need dynamic tools to navigate personal and professional change."

Dr. Joe Macinnis, Oceanographer

We now turn to two architects who could not be more different. The first is a practitioner of marine and submarine evolutionary construction methods: Wolf Hilbertz. This architect tirelessly searched for innovative solutions. The other, Yona Friedman is a theorist of mobile architecture. He shifts his focus to thinking about changeable design methods. He is the inspiring *sparring partner* for a conversation about fluid architecture in the sea. As we saw in the first chapter of our book, one can imagine the sea, its tides, its colors and light scenarios, swarm, write poems, rhyme, as did Saint-John Perse or Pablo Neruda. And one can observe the Oceans as did Claude Lévi-Strauss, who in 1934 was crossing from Marseille to Santos, Brazil, and notes the Sea-Sun-Spectacle, in which the central star first becomes an architect, then a painter: "Every sunset has two distinct phases. In the beginning, the sun plays the role of an architect. Later, when its rays no longer shine directly and are mere reflections, it turns into a painter. As soon as it disappears behind the horizon the light weakens and the complexity of the planes becomes ever greater and greater. Broad daylight is the enemy of perspective, but, between day and night, there is a moment of transition at which the architecture of the skies is as fantastic as it is ephemeral. When darkness comes, everything flattens down again, like some marvelously colored Japanese toy." **60**

60 Claude Lévi-Strauss, *Tristes Tropiques*. Translated by John Russell. (London: Hutchinson, 1961) 69, 70. https://ia800305.us.archive.org/12/items/tristestropiques000177mbp/tristestropiques000177mbp.pdf

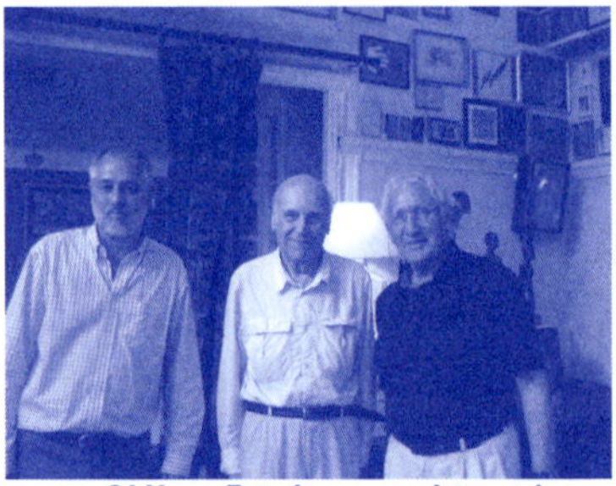

31 Yona Friedman, architect (center), with Roger Marina (left) and Jürgen Claus in the Paris home of the Malinas.

The Planet Ocean spreads out in all its structured splendor. Far away from mythologies, we contemporary discoverers of the energetic *black holes*, see everything scientifically different compared to our ancestors. But despite all the fine electronic devices and instruments, we see the cosmos still with the eyes of the ancestors. The sensual experience of the sea stimulates our designs of the *Gestalt* of the sea.

Fig. 31

I talk about this in Paris with Yona Friedman, a tireless forward-thinker among architects. His Paris apartment, 33 Boulevard Garibaldi, is a work of art in itself, ceilings and walls painted. Yona Friedman does not find it difficult to play through all the conceivable possibilities of Underwater Architecture. I find it difficult to steer him in his flow of thoughts towards something stable, built, solid. Doesn't the refugee in the sea also need a private or intimate room? "But this could be produced almost like a squid. Why not?" Friedman is in his element. Liquid thinking. "A simple process makes part of the water opaque: a bubble mechanism! Walls made of air bubbles. If only the breathing process can be adapted to the water, all other techniques follow by themselves." We change the conditions. We change our thinking as it corresponds to the Planet Ocean, where gravity is not the problem, but lift, weightlessness. "Here on the mainland, we have problems with energy procurement. A submarine system can be maintained with much less energy. Anyway, you can brainstorm through all these aspects by changing the hypothesis." At the end of a long, stimulating conversation, Yona Friedman sums up what interests him about my questions about a possible marine architecture. "There are three areas: The submarine realm as an emigration area; the infrastructure as a truly natural one; the de-mechanization of numerous functions."

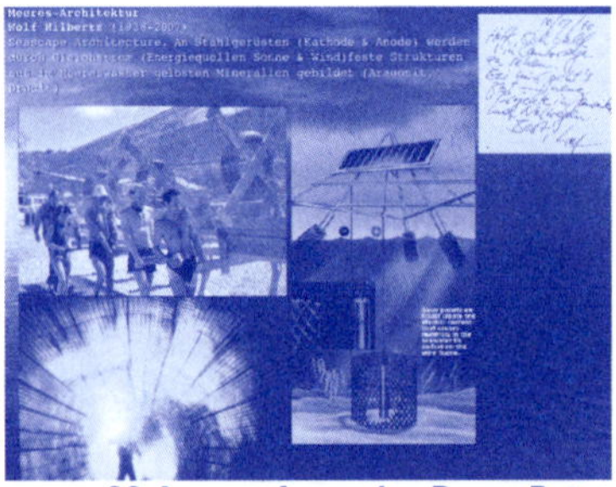

32 A page from the PowerPoint presentation by Jürgen Claus on submarine architecture by Wolf Hilbertz. Shown are clockwise: Hilbertz and his staff insert a wire construction into the sea; solar modules supply the construction with electricity; view into a grid construction below the sea surface. Above right, a message from Hilbertz to the author that he will be on his way to new projects in America and Norway.

Fig. 32

Among the people possessed of the sea was Wolf Hilbertz, a German-Westphalian dickhead who did not give up until his death the dream of Utopia: a self-growing, self-regulating city in the sea. He had risked everything to win everything. He gave up the safe haven of an architecture professorship at the University of Texas in Austin, moved to an island off the Texas coast, Galveston, where he operated the *Marine Resources Company*, undertook the Saya expedition in the Indian Ocean in 2002 with coral specialist Tom Goreau, and then lived in Thailand. His idea was to use the sea as an electrolytic medium. He sank metal grids into the water and connected them to batteries, feeding the electricity from the sun, wind, and tides. Minerals, preferably calcium carbonate and magnesium hydroxide, were deposited on the negatively charged metal grid. Over time, they formed a solid layer. Building materials from seawater: the principle of hope that Wolf Hilbertz set his hopes on. The seemingly strange question: How quickly can you build with seawater?

Within one week, thicknesses of about 0,164 ft can be achieved. However, the material remains brittle and is not properly load-bearing. If the lattice structures remain in the water for months, the material becomes more crystalline, similar to our bones, and very resilient. Hilbertz had already held seminars for architecture students on the Antilles island of St. Croix. Of course, this was unusual at first: Students have to take a diving exam before they can write their doctoral thesis. The long-term goal of these young architects was to use the energies of the natural environment to build an artificial island. For Hilbertz, that would be a total work of art. All aspects of architecture, art, biology, meteorology, etc. intermingled here. And this island should be habitable. I hear the deep, warm voice of Wolf Hilbertz: “We want to found a colony. Children will be born there, and people will develop their own administrative structures. The whole thing is an evolutionary process.” Hilbertz has never given up his marine architecture, has always broken into new areas.

The goal: A marine architecture that is produced without climate impact. It is said that the climate future is decided in the cities. How would it be to ask what the largest areas of our planet, the seas, bays, lagoons, rivers, and the large cities adjacent to them can contribute to this if we combine them with renewable energy concepts? Coral gardens are sensitive ecosystems that have been under constant stress for years due to the constant increase in sea temperature. Coral polyps repel algae when the water temperature rises slightly. One degree Celsius is enough. Polyps and algae form a biocoenosis: algae find fertilizer on corals, but they supply nutrients and energy which they extract from sunlight. The fantastic colors of the corals are the visible result of this fruitful cooperation. If the color splendor decreases, the imminent death of the system is to be expected. Without algae no corals. The so-called bleaching of corals – caused by El Niño, so the well-founded suspicion – led in 1998 to immense damage and the death of entire coral areas. Asia and Australia were particularly affected. Water pollution and aggressive fishing with dynamite and cyanide contribute to the irreversible destruction of coral reefs worldwide.

The *electric coral reef* installed by Wolf Hilbertz and Tom Goreau in North Bali in 2000 was created with the simplest means: On site, on the beach of Pemutaran, the construction iron available on the local market was welded together and sunk into the sea. Then divers tied coral seedlings with thin iron wire to the grids. They had previously collected the seedlings at various points in the sea: small isolated individual pieces broke off by storms and anchors from reefs. The underwater installation was electrified by cables connected to control devices on the shore. In other similar installations, floating solar panels provide the power. Snorkelers and divers can safely touch the structure. The applied voltage is 3 volts at 10-ampere current.

III.5 Ocean Renewable Energies

If one sees marine architectures as possible energy architectures, then today one sails on new terrain, a new sea. Rudimentary architectural approaches are the giant floating islands equipped with solar thermal energy that Thomas Hinderling of the *Swiss Center for Electronics and Microtechnology* **61** not only considered years ago, calculated but also prototypical, financed by the Arab Emirate Ras al-Khaimah with 5 million dollars, had carried out in Dubai. While the large-scale technical implementation is still to come, the idea of using the increased *solar radiation* near the equator in a quiet location at sea remains virulent. The solar island consists of an outer steel ring. Inside it is covered by a foil. An overpressure is generated underneath, with which the weight of the solar panels is stabilized. Small hydrodynamic motors can move the island and avoid unfavorable storms. With a diameter of one mile, a solar island would generate 190 megawatts of power. Although still a long way off, architect Koen Olthuis took up the idea and redesigned it: thousands of solar cells carried by conical buoys on the sea surface.

61 Cf. https://www.csem.ch/home

Sustainable energy for everyone! The initial goal of the UN Solution 2012 was an extremely reduced but globally valid energy requirement of 100 kWh of electricity per person per year. On the other hand, the second target is to convert 40% of global energy consumption to sustainability by 2030. To achieve this alone, an average of 35–40 billion dollars of capital must be raised per year, not including investments in marine architectures. So who pays for them? One of the profitable sustainable energy suppliers at sea are the offshore wind turbines, of which 18,500 megawatts were installed in the world market leader Europe by 2018. A team of architects, who worked together between 2008 and 2010 under the label "on office", combined such offshore wind power plants with residential and exhibition areas, for which the lower floating part of the plants was fully booked: *Turbine City*. Such hybrid architecture and energy plants were proposed for the windy coast off Stavanger in Norway, another attractive model, financially linked to offshore wind farms. *Turbine City*, the fusion of several habitable turbines within a wind farm, would be located in the middle of the open sea and would include a hotel, a museum and wellness facilities. One of these new giant turbines could generate 8 MW, only 1 MW is needed to power the entire facility. Norway's coast could use this economic impulse to reinvent and redefine itself. The coastal cities remain as original as they are – only on the horizon would the turbine city be recognizable.

Fig. 33

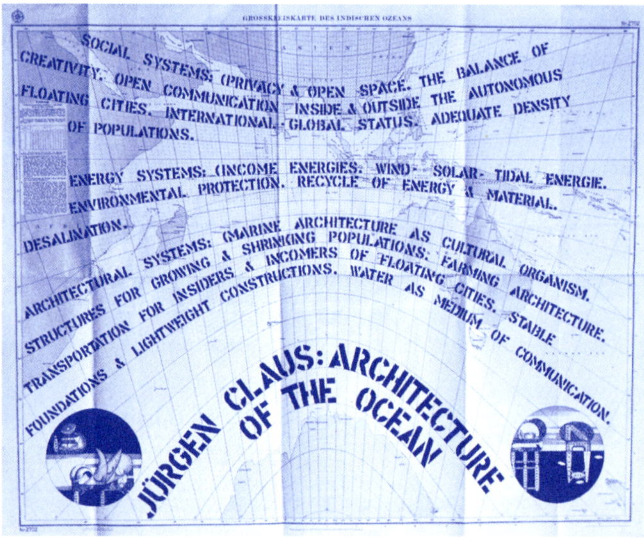

33 Jürgen Claus, Architecture of the Ocean. Ink drawing on navigation chart of the Indian Ocean, 1973. The text presents (from top to bottom) the social systems, the energy systems and the architectural systems.

III.6 Diving and Fluid Realities

III.6.1 Life Experiments:

A Talk with Futurologist

Robert Jungk

Friday, December 10, 1971. Robert Jungk and I have withdrawn to his hermitage in Salzburg, Austria to talk about the Planet Ocean as space of *imagination*. In front of him on the desk, the travel typewriter with the sheet clamped, manuscripts, cigarettes, coffee cups. When I sketched out my thesis on the phone, he had said that he was currently very interested in questions of perception, as well as the expansion of communication systems. So we have a common starting point for the conversation for my book, which is about *Art & Environmental Research Underwater*. Nothing, or almost nothing, is determined by man in the sea. Here is a space for life experiments, and if another society, another culture is to be created, so my thesis, then the artist must also be prepared for his part to question everything that art has secured so far. What does Jungk think of this?

First, a few words about the person sitting across from me. Born in Berlin in 1913 and deceased in Salzburg in 1994, Jungk was and is regarded as one of the most prominent futurologists of the 20th century. A central field of his work was the creation of *future workshops* (*Zukunfts Werkstätten*). New social solutions are to be found in an exchange of different age and occupational groups. This process goes through three phases. In a first process the problems are analyzed. The second stage relies entirely on the imagination; all restrictions are frowned upon. The third phase unfolds the panorama in which the proposed solutions can be implemented.

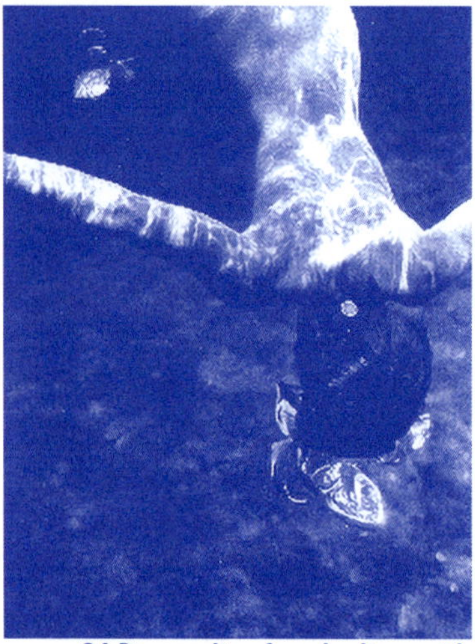
34 Descending female diver with metal flower, Stromboli, 1970.

Jungk is concerned with the question whether man should not finally give up the fiction of the post fixing of the facts *post festum* (afterwards) in order to devote himself above all to the observation of events as long as they are *in flux*. So a person would have to be there at the same time as the event to be observed, and secondly a person would have to accept the constant variability. Perception in the submarine fulfills these two criteria, I argue. One lives in a fluid reality. Jungk takes up the thread. Imagine, he says, that one develops a completely different kind of observation and of language, underwater. You have a much greater sensitivity to gestures, colors and light. What touches us most in water is that we have no routine clues here. This leads to an enormous disorientation. It would be a chance. One could imagine that in contact with the sea, this completely different feeling of not being a master, but a cork – but also part of a much bigger, more comprehensive, more powerful one – develops.

It is contagious, it gives courage to get involved with this man about submarine and sea futures. He designs what is to come, but does not bind. Our visions, he says, are only heuristic instruments, not programs. You then have to add your own things. Because hopefully in the next generation you will already be completely different again. In addition – in this context he also saw my idea of the Planet Ocean – man must open up new experimental fields, which can be *life experiments*.

Fig. 34

This is how I saw the development that leads from the expansion of art to an *expansion of man*, in his entire mental-biological constitution. An art under water, for which I have written and carried out the programme during these years, brings a new beginning, new coordinates, because the space in the sea itself, even if it is only the coastal space, is not yet mapped by our senses. Diving creates that foreignness that is at the same time very intimate. A body is quite sensual, and yet abstract. The body may be so familiar to you from above. Your fingertips feel it through the salt water. The sensation is coarse but changed. You glide along a body by changing your dimension yourself, you may be standing on your head; you glide around a body, no verbal utterance is necessary, you are now completely left to your gestures, your fingertips have to take over the statement, you are seeing and blind at the same time, deaf and full of sensation.

I imagine gardens under water. Floral forms, a thread of glass, you dive through a zone of these leaves floating in the sea, a labyrinth. Another time you come at night, the gardens are illuminated by underwater spotlights. Now is the madness method. You get lost all the time, your orientation is zero, the leaves have no foundation, end below as above, you make a mighty effort not to go mad. This time you are stuck in an acoustic zone. The loudspeakers circle. You begin to define a foreign space. A space made up only of music, sounds, noises. The sea at night has no other landmarks than the acoustic ones. No light. A school in which you forget to unfold your usual terms and then determine practice. Your behavior is determined by this. You are the pacemaker of yourself.

I have transmitted my diving enthusiasm to Robert Jungk. The fantasy, he confirms to me, is the big yeast. The true revolution would be to break the suppression of fantasy. We should risk giving up the mainland of solid truths over and over again to discover new territory in the sea of countless possibilities.

"Oceanology may seem a subject which has little in common with the preoccupations of modern art. But I doubt if this will be so for long, because of its almost unequaled appeal to the imagination."

Farooq Hussain, Studio International, 1969

Fig. 35

The young diver and scientist Dr. Hans Hass had written once "Do not forget to emerge!" on a metal plate, because the diving supply via oxygen, as usual in early times of diving technology, led easily to deep intoxication. There you could see everything in the water more emphatically, bigger anyway. So what a terrain for an art that can be weightless, that can hardly make the diver connected to the device breathless, but speechless – and that also applies to diving art lovers. I had my underwater studios of the early nineteen-seventies in front of the Lipari island Stromboli or the Cyclades island Ios, always within sight of barren but fantastic rock structures that offered a sharp contrast to the rather minimalist art device. Important to me were the bodies that formed the caryatids of a liquid architecture naked in the water, a few meters below the surface. In Wolf Huber's Munich photo laboratory, we solarized the bodies we took, adding virtuality to reality.

Fig. 36

I published the results, together with a mosaic of future projects, in my book *Planet Ocean. Art & Environmental Research under Water*, which appeared in the DuMont Programme in 1972, and shortly afterward in Mexico in Spanish. I was looking for allies, like poet, painter, film-

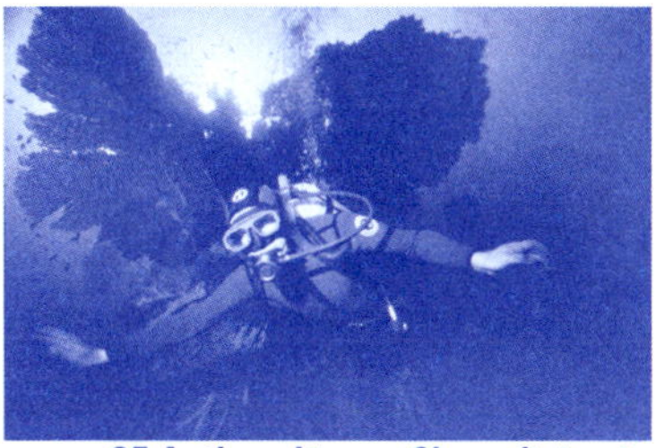

35 Author Jürgen Claus diving in the Coral Gardens of the Red Sea.

maker Jean Cocteau, who said to his diving partner Yves Le Prieur in 1926: "You have discovered what the future holds for me. The princes of your kingdom are Leonardo and Jules Verne." His diving experience was later incorporated into Cocteau's film interpretations of mirrors and their passage. In the contemporary of the sixties, I only knew of an artist friend who made installations in the sea with natural objects such as floating calabashes or plants: that was the American Peter Hutchinson. In the meantime, some have been added. When mentioning the diving body, one may remember Fernand Léger with his *Divers on a yellow background* (1941, at the Art Institute Chicago) or the *Multicolored Divers* (1942–46, at the Léger Museum in Biot). One day Léger went to a bathing establishment in the USA. He could no longer tell who this head, this leg and this arm belonged to. So he mixed up the limbs in his pictures.

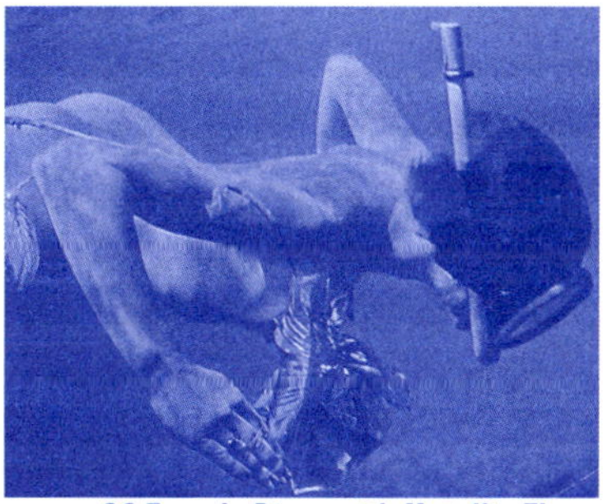

36 Female Diver with Metallic Flower at the coastline of Stromboli, 1970.

The *Expansion of Art*, as my book from 1970 was called and my artistic goal and program were to be described, led from the painted underwater scene to the real, no longer only imagined sculpture, installation, and performance in the sea. It is a kind of field research of art and by the artist. How this takes place will be described in the following by means of a protocol. I try to trace a dive to artistic sculptures with words.

Jump into the sea. The left hand reaches for the diving goggles, with the right hand I press three underwater cameras against my life jacket. Ten feet below the surface of the water I turn my body, which is covered in a multitude of technical aids. I am in my element, the planet sea, a *liquid planet*. There's twilight on land now. The setting sun has left a tableau of yellow, ochre and red in the sky. In the water itself a pierced blue. Visibility about 33 feet. I dive down. Pressure compensation by swallowing. 23 feet depth, 26 feet. I let some air into the life jacket and stabilize at this depth. A panorama. Above the dark blue surface of the hull. Two divers, who descended with me, in the distance. 33 feet below me the seabed, which is flat here. Small shoals of fish. This is not all that interests me, what drove me to this dive and the countless others in the last days.

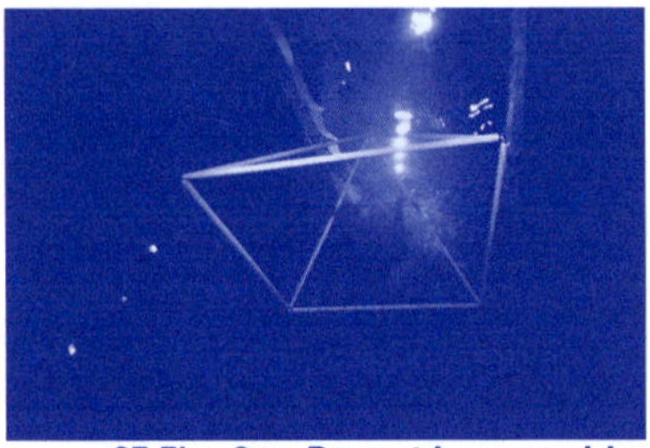

37 The Sun Pyramid, created by Jürgen Claus, shines in the sea. Solar modules on the sea surface feed the Artwork with renewable energy.

The *Sun Pyramid* it is! Light from sunlight. It floats 33 feet away from me. A square pyramid whose edges consist of 10 feet long fluorescent tubes. Its yellow-green light cuts a clearly defined shape into infinite blue. Even hours after sunset the sun pyramid will still shine under water. A total of 16 solar modules, each measuring 3'3" to 2'2", have collected the energy of the light on the water surface with their photovoltaic cells and conducted it to a battery, which now supplies the Sun Pyramid with electricity. Three points of light appear near our dive boat. They will soon unfold glistening light next to and inside the pyramid. I had asked four divers to dive in with magnesium torches. They still have to wait at the surface until the torches have unfolded their full power. Now they dive in. Almost vertically, holding the torches with their knitted hands in front of them, they drift towards the four sides of the Sun Pyramid. The water gives off a fascinating, wide reflex body for the radiant light. At the same time the two divers, who were already in the water, switch on their hand lights. We changed them with red filters in front of the glass. Now the whole play of light is going on. The pyramid, torches, portable spotlights – light in the sea, transient, but renewable in the fluorescent tubes, connected to the cycle of natural sunlight. I'm trying to control my enthusiasm. In the viewfinder of the camera appears the scene as two-dimensional image. Now it's time to react quickly, to shoot after shooting.

Fig. 37–38

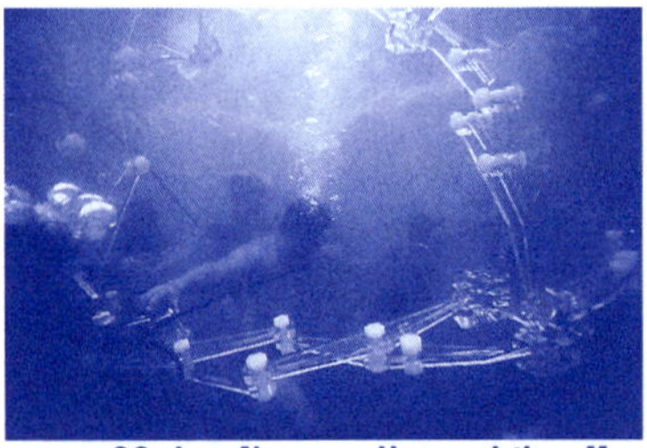

38 Jun Nguyen-Hatsushiba, *Memorial Project Minamata: Neither Either nor Neither–A Love Story*, 2003, Still from Video.

I am now after the pioneer days of the 1960s and 1970s, not quite alone as an artist in the sea. There's the Japanese Jun Nguyen-Hatsushiba who lives in Vietnam. He brings turbulent underwater installations with intoxicating people diving up and down into the picture, i.e. into the video and photography. His works, which have a strong social context, occasionally flash at international biennials and triennials. "Towards the Complex" premiered in 2001. Half a dozen free divers move bicycle taxis on the seabed. In another memorial project from 2003, traditional dragon dolls were moved. A wheel of fortune throws balls of color upwards, which discolor the water. In all the gigantic motion sequences, the divers cross out, the soundtracks convey frightening noises: Vietnam's sorrowful story cries out! Underwater is really here, as the Japanese language says better than ours: Inside the water.

The American Doug Aitken is one of the artists who has gone out to sea and underwater with their works. He discovered a small, still intact ecotope on the Pacific island of Catalina, one hour away from the Californian mainland. The chewing gum heir William Wrigley had bought the island in 1919 and transferred his shares in 1975 to an environmental foundation, which today owns almost 90% of the island. No better place to draw attention to the conservation of the sea with artistic structures. Doug Aitken had his artistic breakthrough with the film *Diamond Sea*, shot in 1997 in abandoned diamond mines, received the International Prize of Venice in 1999 for his video installation *Electric Earth*. In 2007, passers-by walked through huge projection surfaces in Manhattan, sleepwalking (*Sleepwalkers*), fading in the privacy of the anonymity of the skylines. Aitken artistically challenges all media, including a U.S. train that traveled 4.038 miles from the Atlantic to the Pacific and before which nomadic happenings were staged at ten public locations in September 2013.

Raised in Redondo Beach, for Aitken the Pacific Ocean is the other essential side of the planet. So there is nothing more obvious than to include this fluid medium as well. He designed three dodecagonal, open pavilions mirrored on some sides (Latin: *papilio* = butterfly). A local boat builder and assistants created the bodies, which were anchored in the sea at various depths off Catalina Island until the middle of 2016, an experience for divers, visible to those arrested by a series of underwater cameras. The pavilions became *living systems*, as Doug Aitken sees it, lenses and gates into the underwater world.

Now Cyrill Gutsch comes into the (sponsor) game. He had left Munich, Germany for New York, had been relegated to the planet sea by the environmental pioneer Paul Watson, had founded *Parley for the Oceans* and found in Aitken the addressee of his commitment to a reorientation of maritime policy. Each generation fights its own battles. Goals overlap. In the 1970s, I had met and worked with Elizabeth Mann-Borgese, a marine activist. She had provided the drama of the sea with a comprehensive book scenario. She saw the seas as our great laboratory, also for peace, *Pacem in Maribus*, as her engagement was called. In those years Captain Cousteau had also become an environmental activist. In 1981, in New York, he told me: “The sea gives us the receipt for what we do to it.”

Gutsch’s partnership with Aitken and finally the MOCA in Los Angeles created the *pavilions*. The eco-standards calculated how much material and energy was consumed to produce the submerging butterflies and offset that against the environmental consciousness to be achieved. If it were quantifiable, tens of thousands of people who share the emphatic ocean experience via the net, among other things, would nevertheless have to be counted as a positive weight.

III.8 Sound Structures Experienced Underwater

The sound of the spheres had become obsolete. John Cage did not want to hear any more music. He found them around him, heard them everywhere and anytime. That was in 1973 when the Canadian Murray Schafer had already founded his *World Soundscape Project* and roamed lakes, forests and cities with mobile recording devices to document *Nada Brahma*, the sound of the world, as Joachim-Ernst Berendt presented it in 1983 as audio art and book. If the range of hearing is so much wider than that of vision, we will also have to work with our ears in the fields of anthropology, evolution, and linguistics – as we have done with our eyes for millennia. Now, says an increasing number of sound researchers, we must finally experience the planet ocean, earth and biosphere in general as a sound field, register it, develop it artistically and understand it better. We have to get used to the fact that sounds and not pictures occupy exhibitions, museums, galleries, which has serious consequences for the art (sound) trade of the sound (art) property. Who owns the sounds of the earth and its inhabitants? Is there retention of title for the sound cosmos of the whales?

The Norwegian sound artist Jana Winderen uses sounds of marine organisms as source material for compositions. *Ultrafield,* for example, uses sounds that are not accessible to the human ear, but with which living creatures in the sea communicate. These real-life sounds, captured in Madeira or Kaliningrad, among other places, are then "booted up" with special sound software, making them accessible to us. Under the title *Sounding: a contemporary score* the sound work was presented at the MOMA, New York, 2013. Those who want to be fascinated by the acoustic world in the oceans can do so via the LIDO ("Listen to the Deep Ocean Environment") software, a global association of research institutes led by the Technical University of Catalonia in Barcelona. This is the raw and compositional basic material – remarkable enough in itself – for sound artists worldwide, such as Yolande Harris, whose sound works could be experienced in Frankfurt's Schirn Museum. Listening to the ocean in the desert: a confrontation of different ecologies, as Philippe Diolé, a diver and writer from the Cousteau team, had raised in 1955. At the beginning of his book on *The Most Beautiful Desert in the World*, he describes what sounds like a preface to Harris's sound installation, the magical operation of dissolving time and space in the sea as in the desert. Yolande Harris de-contextualizes the two extreme spaces by making their sound and image renderings emphatically experienceable for us.

Hundreds of artists around the world have set out to define and practice the politics of sound art in a self-aware and responsible manner. Increasingly, the ecological or biospheric question arises: what does hearing the earth mean for its continued existence? The books that are published in the USA are legion, and underpin the intensive discourse in school education, at universities, in innovative network cooperation. For about 30years, *Leonardo's Music Journal* in Oakland has been a compendium of the sound researching and sound practicing community; for more than 25 years, the *Journal of Acoustic Ecology* has bundled the questions that arise between sound, nature, and society. Hans Joachim Berendt in 1985: "He who has ears to hear sees!"

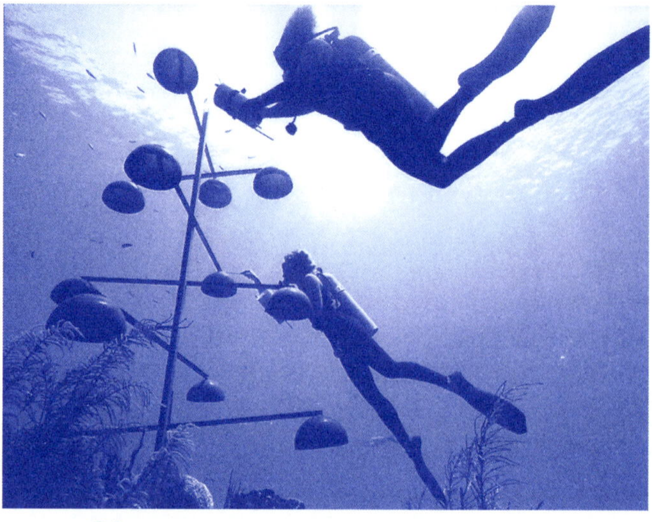

39 Jürgen Claus, *Bell Tower under Water*. Divers play the Bell Tower, which is temporarily installed under water in a reef of the Bahamas island Long Island.

III.8.1 A Bell Tower lowered into the Ocean

Fig. 39

The idea of a Submarine Center took hold of the author at the end of the 1960s. Like many other artists, he had rebuffed the art market, focusing instead on reworking his book, *Expansion of Art*. **62** By 1969, he had finished a blueprint for a *Submarine Center*, which was composed of three sections: an audiovisual center, a center for theory and research, and an experimental diving center. **63** Like a cybernetic system, these three parts were closely linked. In the following short synopsis, the focus is on the concept of the audiovisual center, which included sound art. Although written 50 years ago, the book from 1972, *Planet Ocean. Art & Environmental Research Underwater* captures the concept precisely. It expresses an early concept of environmentally created sound art, but its view of the project is as relevant today as it was then. It states:

62 Jürgen Claus, *Expansion der Kunst. Action – Environment – Kybernetik – Technik – Urbanistik*. (Reinbek/Hamburg: Rowohlt, 1970.) A Spanish edition came out as *Expansión del arte*. (Mexico: Editorial Extemporaneos, 1970); a Japanese translation was published in1972 by Shakei-Shi-Sho, Tokyo.

63 Cf. page 50.

"The sound world of the seas. Their spatial restoration. A whole library of this sound world has been assembled since 1946 by the Narragansett Marine Laboratory of the University of Rhode Island: *The Reference File of Biological Underwater Sounds*. **64** The sound material in the audiovisual center can be handled, processed, set free, manipulated, superimposed, recorded, stored, reproduced by anyone. On the one hand, mechanical sound devices are available for this purpose. On the other hand, electronic devices. Finally, as a third sound group, recordings from the submarine space are available. Special emphasis is placed on the experience of sound processing. PROCESS MUSIC. PROCESS SOUND STRUCTURES."

64 Of particular importance is the recovery of the original recordings of fish sounds that accompanied the landmark book *Sounds of Western North Atlantic Fishes* by Marie Fish and William Mowbray (1970). They examined 218 species from 59 families, and found biological sounds from 153 species from 36 families. "We have created a CD-ROM containing digital copies of sound clips from 171 species that produced sounds (both biological and incidental) as published in Fish and Mowbray 1970. We characterized each species as having weak (83), moderately (37) and strong (47) sound production (4 undetermined). Only 47 species from 24 families were observed to produce truly spontaneous sounds (no mechanical or electrical stimulation). Although Fish and Mowbray include 160 sonograms and 329 oscillograms, they fail to provide summaries of acoustic parameters such as frequency range, peak, amplitude, pulse rate, number of pulses per call, call duration, etc. We anticipate that this type of information would be included in a new National Archive of Fish Sounds" http://www.fishecology.org/soniferous/soundpub2.htm (May 15, 2018)

For the *Submarine Center*, the author designed a "walk-in" diving sphere that was to be 33 feet high and half-filled with water. (Cf. p. 50) Above, it had a platform, which doubled as a changing room and included a unit for insights, information, and communication. From this platform, the art lover, equipped with underwater breathing apparatus and diving suit, would descend into the sphere and enter the water. There, underwater, the diver would experience a new world of the acoustics of different qualities and nuances.

During a film shoot of *Planet Ocean. Underwater Art by Jürgen Claus* in 1979, Claus explored another special artistic experience with underwater sound. **65** One of the central motifs of the film was a bell tower lowered into the ocean to a depth of about 15 meters. This idea came to him on the Greek island of Serifos. From the parched ground of that arid environment, plants emerged with white, bell-like flowers, the stimulus to create a bell tower in the sea. The bell tower was filmed among the reefs of Long Island, Bahamas. It comprised a total of 12 bells of bright orange-colored glass suspended from an aluminum structure. The bell tower was at one and the same time a sculpture and an instrument played by divers with underwater flares in their hands. (Cf. Fig. 39) All of our premises on land are destined for sound: we build rooms in a dimension in which we can communicate with each other. Under water, this is completely different. One can imagine the underwater space of the sea as a huge concert hall. The association was perhaps best expressed in the poems of Pablo Neruda in which he counts the bells living in the sea and their ringing in the sea. ("... quiero estar solo con el mar principal y la campana.") **66**

65 Cf. https://www.youtube.com/watch?v=LZCOQgZN-YA

66 "I want to be alone with the first-born sea and the Bell". (Pablo Neruda, *Letzte Gedichte*. Spanish and German (Munich: Luchterhand, 1975.) p. 171.

"More than 200 million people currently live on land that could be flooded by sea level rise by the end of the century."

Woods Hole Oceanographic Institution

The concept of floating energy islands was the object of speculation as far back as 1881, by the way, when French physicist Jacques-Arsène d'Arsonval (1851–1940) considered the idea. Today, so-called ocean thermal energy conversion (OTEC) technology is one of the great hopes of renewable energy. Former Siemens R&D head Wolfgang Volkrodt patented a self-supporting floating solar foil technology in 1989. Such an island, Volkrodt believed, could have been built within two years at a cost (at the time) of Deutsche Mark 6 billion (± 3 billion Euros) and would have had a capacity comparable to a nuclear power plant. A hybrid structure of energy islands which combines wind power, photovoltaics, solar thermal, and hydrogen production might have the best prospects for the future. Someone even calculated that 53,000 energy islands of this type, with 74 MW of capacity each and taking up only 42.857 square yards of the ocean, would cover the energy demand of the world's entire population.

A project like *Autopia*, the energy self-sufficient city, once proposed by Wolf Hilbertz, asks how the largest areas of the planet – seas, bays, lagoons, and rivers – can be used to develop sustainable energy concepts for these areas. Concrete action is needed. The World Bank has demonstrated that countries with inadequate energy systems lose one to two percent of their growth each year. "Water is the next big thing," says Dutch water architect Koen Olthuis, who presented with Davis Keuning the book manifesto *Float* in 2010. Water for the problems of the megacities on the continental margins of the oceans. All ninety of the hundred largest cities in the world settle on water. Already at the end of the 1950s, the sea was included in the architects' plans. The American William Katavolos, introduced a settlement on the sea in 1960, floating on rings of oil products into which chemical substances were poured. Katavolos predicted a "polymeric revolution" that anticipated many parts of the current nanoworld. As a diver he came into close contact with the sea, as a visionary, he wrote: "In the morning you can see settlements that join together to form cities, to float like sounds into the distance towards evening, to anchor themselves somewhere else". **67** This is the architect speaking, 1960. More than 60 years after his statement, it is encouraging to see an imagination of marine architecture blossoming.

67 William Katavolos, „Organics", in: Ulrich Conrads, *Programs and manifestoes on the 20th-century architecture.* (Cambridge, Massachusetts: MIT Press.) 164

"A new architecture is possible through the matrix of chemistry. Man must stop making and manipulating, and instead allow architecture to happen. There is a way beyond building just as the principles of waves, parabolas and plummet lines exist beyond the mediums in which they form. So must architecture free itself from the traditional patterns and become organic. [...]

Visualize the new city grow molded on the sea, of great circles of oil substances producing patterns in which plastics pour to form a network of strips and discs that expand into toruses and spheres, and further perforate for many purposes. Double walls are windowed in new ways containing chemicals to heat, to cool, and to clean, ceiling patterns created like crystals, floors formed like corals, surfaces structurally ornamented with visible stress patterns that leap weightlessly above us. The fixed floors provide the paraphernalia for a living, a vast variety of disposable pods plugged into more permanent cellular cells." **68**

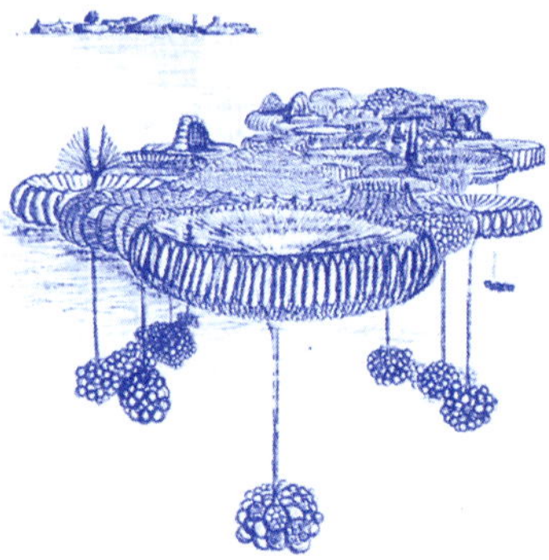

40 William Katavolos. Sketch of a floating seaside city made of changeable materials.

68 Ibid. 163.

Fig. 40

I'm already close to my favorite idea of the book. *To the Oceans with Imagination* means to leave the fixed traces of experience. My book began with the question if one can understand the sea, the oceans, as a *medium*, as the subtitle suggests. The last sentences take up this question again. Is the ocean a medium for scuba-diving humans? Just like photography or film or video are a medium? If one simply accepts these premises, then the following becomes apparent:

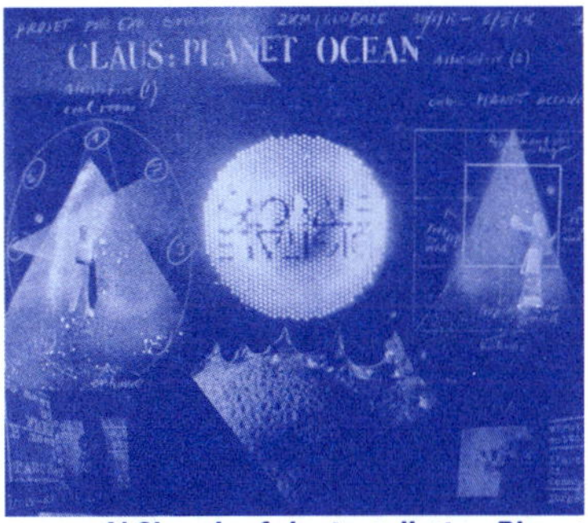

41 Sketch of the installation *Planet Ocean* by Jürgen Claus, proposed for the *Globale* Exhibition 2015 at ZKM, Karlsruhe, Germany.

having dived into the primal energy of an element like water, the carrying or documenting medium (photography, film, video, etc.) comes to be of little importance. How should it convey temperature, skin contact, the experience of movement? But then in reverse: enclosed in the post-processing facility of the video-editing site, the medium counts for a lot, indeed for everything. The fictitious reality of the medium has an authoritarian or at least defining, determining impact.

Media are mirrors that possess the strange magic of preserving the images which they take up in the appearance of realities, at least for a certain time. They are the pieces of coal in memory. They are fossils, actually something that has died of which, however, energy can be derived. Media unfold a new reality which, for its part, is capable of being treated in artistic terms. And this, in turn, is artistically processable. So: *Salute to the media!* They can hardly ferment in the book. Here they are like bacteria waiting for other plantations to grow and show themselves.

Perhaps one can say that media today get a musical, a performative context: their (half-dead) scores kindle themselves in the act of experience, the media reality lies in the resonance of the experiencer, in the wave range in which the energies exchange, overlap, communicate. This is an art far beyond the screens and the cool prints of photographs and films. The energy zone determines the value of the medium. It is the concert hall of the medium, at the same time its performance and its experience.

Fig. 41

Books, AV-Material *(Selection)*

A

AA, l'architecture d'aujourd'hui, "Living in the Sea", 1974
'A'A', l'architecture d'aujourd'hui, 427, October 2018
Akel, Matthias Josef (ed.), Doug Aitken. (Vienna: Verlag für moderne Kunst, 2015) Alam Deohttps://www.youtube.com/watch?v=bGuS6GULGqE

B

Banham, Reyner, *Megastructure. Urban Futures of the Recent Past.* (London: Thames and Hudson, 1976.)
Barsky, Steven M., *Underwater Digital Video Made Easy*, (Springfield, Missouri: Hammerhead Press, 2005)
Berendt, Joachim-Ernst, *Das Dritte Ohr. Vom Hören der Welt*, (Reinbeck bei Hamburg: Rowohlt, 1985) English: *The Third Ear. On Listening to the World. Foreword by Yehudi Menuhin*, (Longmead, Shaftesbury, Dorset: Element Books, 1988)
Boeckmann, Kurt von, *Vom Kulturreich des Meeres*. (Berlin: Wegweiser-Verlag, 1924)
Bureaud, Annick, *water is in the air. Physics, Politics, and Poetics of Water in the Arts*. (Cambridge, MA: Leonardo ebook series, MIT Press, Kindle Edition by Irit Batsry.) 2014

C

Callebaut, Vincent, *Archibiotic*. In Chinese.
Callebaut, Vincent, *Fertile Cities*. Design Media Publishing Ltd., 2015.
Callebaut, Vincent, Paris 2050: *Les cités fertiles face aux du enjeux du XXIe siècle*. (Paris: Design Media Pub, 2015) In English.
Claus, Jürgen, *Planet Meer. Kunst & Umweltforschung Unterwasser*. (Cologne: DuMont Schauberg, 1972)
Claus, Jürgen, *Liebe die Kunst*. (Berlin: Kerber, 2015)
Claus, Jürgen, *Der Raum des Meeres. Kunst/Architektur/Forschung*. (Aachen: project claus, 2018)
Claus, Jürgen, PLANET OCEAN, artists video. https://www.youtube.com/watch?v=LZCOQgZN-YA
Cousteau, Jacques, *The Silent World*. (Washington: National Geographic, 2004) First Publication 1954.
Cousteau, Jacques, *Pacific Explorations*. Cousteau Collection. DVD
Cousteau, Jacques, River Explorations. DVD
Cousteau, Jacques and Susan Schiefelbein, *The Human, the Orchid and the Octopus. Exploring and Conserving our Nature World*. (New York: Bloomsbury, 2007.)
Jacques Cousteau's Voyage to the Edge of the World. DVD

E

Earle, Sylvia & Al Giddings (1980). *Exploring the Deep Frontier: The Adventure of Man in the Sea*. (Washington: National Geographic Society, 1980)
Earle, Sylvia & Linda K. Glover, *Ocean: An Illustrated Atlas. (National Geographic Atlas, 2008)*.
Earle, Sylvia A., and Glover, Linda K., (ed.) *Ocean. An Illustrated Atlas*. (Washington: National Geographic, 2009)
World Ocean's Day: Blue heart – an interview with Dr. Sylvia Earle. https://www.youtube.com/watch?v=6PQ6B-mXusGM

F

Flechter, Mark, *Islands. Contemporary architecture on water*. (Königswinter/Potsdam: h.f.ullmann/Tandem, 2009)
Frobenius, Leo, *Vom Kulturreich des Festlandes*. (Berlin: Wegweiser-Verlag, 1923)

G

Giesler, Ulla (ed.), *Water. Curse or blessing!?*. (Berlin: Aedes, 2011)
Guggenheim, Davis, with Al Gore and Billy West, *An Inconvenient Truth*. (2010), DVD

H

Hussain, Farooq, *Living Underwater*. (New York: Praeger, 1970.)

K

Kurokawa, Kisho, *Metabolism in Architecture*. (Durrington: Littlehampton Book Services Ltd, 1977)

L

Latour, Bruno, *Down to Earth. Politics in the New Climate Regime*. (Cambrigde, UK: Polity, 2018)
Leggewie, Claus, *Zukunft im Süden. Wie die Mittelmeerunion Europa wiederbeleben kann*. (Hamburg: Edition Körber-Stiftung, 2012)

M

Machu, Franck, *Frédéric Dumas*.
Madsen, Brad, *Jacques Cousteau. The Sea King*. (New York: Random House, 2009)
MacInnis, Joe (Foreword by Pierre Elliot Trudeau), *Underwater Man*. (New York: Dodd, Mead & Company, 1975)
MacInnis, Joe, *Breathing Underwater: The Quest to Live in the Sea*. (Toronto: Penguin Canada, 2004)
Metabolism. City of the Future. The Proposal for New Urbanism. By Noboru Kawazoe, Kiyonori Kikutake, Masato Otaka, Fumihiko Maki, Kisho Kurokawa. (Tokyo: Bijutsu Shuppanansha, 1960)
Mostafavi, Mohsen with Doherty, Gareth, *Ecological Urbanism*. (Baden/Switzerland: Lars Müller, 2010/2011)

N

Nguyen-Hatsushiba, Jun, *The Globe Project: The Garden of Globes*. Catalogue. (Beijing: Mizuma and One Gallery, 2008)
Nguyen-Hatsushiba, Jun, in: *A Reunion with the Sea: Realism as Modern Asian Thought*. (Okinawa: Prefectural Museum & Art Museum, 2017/2018.)

O

OMA, a-practical-guide-to-a-prosperous-low-carbon-europe.pdf
OMA, *Zeekracht. A masterplan for a renewable energy infrastructure in the North Sea.* 2008. https://oma.eu/publications/zeekracht-a-strategy-for-masterplanning-the-north-sea
OMA, https://atlasofplaces.com/Zeekracht-OMA
Oshima, Ken Tadashi (ed.), *Kiyonori Kikutake – Between Land and Sea.* (Zurich: Lars Müller, 2016.)

P

Perse, Saint-John, *Seamarks.* Bilingual Edition (New York: Harper & Bros, 1961)

R

Ragon, Michel, *prospective et futurologie,* tome 3, nouvelle edition. (Paris: Casterman, 1986)
Raisbeck, Peter, *Marine Cities 1960 to 1975.* Society of Architectural Historians of Australia and New Zealand, October, 2002.
Randerson, Janine, *Weather as Medium. Towar a Meterelogical Art.* (Cambridge; MIT Press,2018)
Rougerie, Jacques, *habiter la mer*, Paris: EMOM, 1978
Rougerie, Jacques, *A Different Life Style. Vivre Autrement.*
Rougerie, Jacques, *De Vingt mille lieues sous les mers à SeaOrbiter.* (Paris: Democratic Books, 2010)

S

Schmitt, Carl: Land und Meer. Eine weltgeschichtliche Betrachtung, (Leipzig: Philipp Reclam, 1942)
Schmitt, Carl: Land and Sea, translated and with a foreword by Simona Draghici. (Washington DC: Plutarch Press, 1997.)
Schmitt, Carl: The Nomos of the Earth in the International Law of the Jus Publicum Europaeum, translated by G. L. Ulmen. (New York: Telos Press, 2006.

T

Toop, David, *Ocean of Sound. Aether Talk, Ambient Sound and Imaginary Worlds.* (Bevin Way: Serpent's Tail, 1995, 2001)

U

UN Global environmental outlook 2019.
https://www.unenvironment.org/resources/global-environment-outlook-6

W

Wietschel, Martin; Ullrich, Sandra; Markewitz, Peter; Schulte, Friedrich; Genoese, Dabio (ed.), *Energietechnologie der Zukunft.* (Wiesbaden: Springer, 2015)
Willemin, Véronique, *maisons sur l'eau*, (Paris: Editions Alternatives, 2008)

Institutions for Further Inquiry (Selection)

The followings texts in *italics* correspond to the self-portrayal of the respective institutions.

American Academy of Underwater Sciences, PO Box 9067, Mobile, AL 36691-9067, Phone: (251) 591-3775, aaus@aaus.org
The mission of the American Academy of Underwater Sciences (AAUS) is to advance and facilitate safe and productive scientific diving. The AAUS was officially chartered in California in 1983 by individuals and organizations involved in the effort to obtain the scientific diving exemption from OSHA commercial diving standards. In the years since, the AAUS has expanded from the original six organizational members to more than 130 organizational members and over 1100 individual members. Organizational membership includes colleges and universities, government agencies, museums and aquaria, environmental and archaeological consulting firms, and community science groups sharing a common thread of the use of diving as a research tool and a commitment to the health and safety of scientific divers. AAUS produces consensual standards for the training and certification of scientific divers and the operation of scientific diving programs, maintains statistics detailing scientific diving activities and incident rates, conducts annual symposia and topical workshops, and directly supports student research.
https://www.aaus.org/

Jean-Michel Cousteau's Ocean Futures Society, 513 De La Vina Street, Santa Barbara, CA 93101,USA. Phone: (805) 899-8899; contact@oceanfutures.org
Honoring his heritage of ocean exploration and protection, Jean-Michel founded Ocean Futures Society in 1999 to carry on this pioneering work. Ocean Futures Society is a non-profit marine conservation and education organization, and serves as a "Voice for the Ocean" by communicating in all media the critical bond between people and the sea and the importance of wise environmental policy. As Ocean Futures' spokesman, Jean-Michel serves as an impassioned diplomat for the environment, reaching out to the public through a variety of media.
http://www.oceanfutures.org; contact@oceanfutures.org

Fabien Cousteau Learning Center, 161 East 35th Street, New York, NY 10016, USA, Tel: (917) 657-9678; http://www.fabiencousteauolc.orgabien
The Fabien Cousteau Ocean Learning Center ("OLC") was founded in 2016 as a 501(c)(3) by world renowned oceanographic explorer, conservationist and documentary filmmaker Fabien Cousteau to fulfill his dream of creating a vehicle for positive change in the world.

Global Underwater Explorers, 18487 High Springs Main Street, High Springs, FL 32643, USA

National Park Service, Department of the Interior, 1849 C Street, N.W., Washington DC 20240; Phone: (202) 208-3100; https://www.doi.gov/contact-us
The National Park Service is a bureau of the U.S. Department of the Interior and is led by a *Director* nominated by the President and confirmed by the U.S. Senate. The Director is supported by senior executives who manage national programs, policy, and budget in the Washington, DC, headquarters and seven regional directors responsible for national park management and program implementation. *The Maritime Heritage Program is part of the National Park Service's Park History Program. For centuries, Americans have used waterways for commerce, transportation, defense, and recreation. The Maritime Heritage Program works to advance awareness and understanding of the role of maritime affairs in the history of the United States. Through leadership, assistance, and expertise in maritime history, preservation, and archeology we help to interpret and preserve our maritime heritage by maintaining inventories of historic U.S. maritime properties, providing preservation assistance through publications and consultation, educating the public about maritime heritage through our website, sponsoring maritime heritage conferences and workshops, and funding maritime heritage projects when grant assistance* is available.

Ocean University of China, 23 Eastern Hongkong Road (OUC Fushan Campus), Qingdao, China, Tel: +86-532-85901555 (English) http://eweb.ouc.edu.cn/2851/list.htm mail: iec@mail.ouc.edu.cn
Ocean University of China (OUC) is a comprehensive university with particular strengths in oceanography and fisheries science. We have four campuses – Yushan, Fushan, Laoshan and Huangdao, which is currently under construction – all of which are united under our motto "Ocean embraces all streams; exploring promises reaching far." The university is proud to be the cradle of China's marine professionals and it counts a large number of China's marine science specialists among its alumni. 70% of China's PhD holders in oceanography and fisheries graduated from OUC; in addition, the first scientist to reach the South Pole, the first Chinese scientist to investigate the South Pole on foot, and the first Chinese scientist to reach both the North and South Poles all graduated from OUC. OUC alumni also comprise 68% of the winners of the National Foundation Awards for Distinguished Young Researchers in Oceanography and 46% of the winners of the National Foundation Awards for Distinguished Young Researchers in fisheries.

Oceanographic Institutions and Programs worldwide https://en.wikipedia.org/wiki/List_of_oceanographic_institutions_and_programs https://en.wikipedia.org/wiki/List_of_oceanographic_institutions_and_pro

Royal Navy Submarine Museum, https://en.wikipedia.org/wiki/Royal_Navy_Submarine_Museum
The new museum complex opened in August 1981 with HMS Alliance as the principal exhibit. Over the years since, more submarines and submarine memorabilia have been added to the collection. In 1983 the museum gained a new display building and members of the public were allowed into HMS Alliance. In 2001 the museum opened a climate-controlled building that houses Holland 1. Visitors to the museum can tour HMS Alliance with a submariner guide, explore the interactive science gallery, step on board the Royal Navy's first submarine Holland I (built in 1901), or wander around the museum exhibits.

The Ocean Policy Research Institute, The Sasakawa Peace Foundation Bldg.1-15-16 Toranomon, Minato-ku, Tokyo,105-8524, Japan,Tel: +81-3-5157-5210, Fax: +81-3-5157-5230.
Since 2000, the Ocean Policy Research Institute, formerly known as the Ocean Policy Research Foundation, has worked as a think tank which aims for a harmonious

Image Credits

relationship between mankind and the oceans through ocean policy research, policy recommendations and publication of information. The Institute also contributed to the enactment of the 2007 Basic Act on Ocean Policy. Since then, the Institute has actively participated in international conferences and debates on ocean governance, and has conducted a number of activities to materialize and promote the implementation of 12 Basic Policies Measures on the ocean as stipulated in the Basic Act on Ocean Policy. Having inherited the activities, human resources, knowledge and networks of the Ocean Policy Research Foundation, the Ocean Policy Research Institute will build upon the Foundation's legacy by conducting research, communication and collaboration as well as publicizing information on the oceans, both in Japan and overseas.

Woods Hole Oceanographic Institution, 266 Woods Hole Road, Woods Hole, MA 02543-1050 USA. Founded in 1930, the WHOI gets Government grants and contracts, foundation and private donations, industry contracts. Annual operating budget of $215 million (2018). Ships: Global Class research vessel *Atlantis*, Ocean Class research vessel *Neil Armstrong*, coastal vessel *Tioga*, small boats. Underwater Vehicles: Human-occupied submersible *Alvin*; Remotely Operated Vehicle (ROV) *Jason/Medea*; Autonomous Underwater Vehicle (AUV) *Sentry*; additional hybrid ROVs, Autonomous Underwater Vehicles, and towed vehicles.
Woods Hole Oceanographic Institution is the world's leading, independent non-profit organization dedicated to ocean research, exploration, and education. Our scientists and engineers push the boundaries of knowledge about the ocean to reveal its impacts on our planet and our lives. WHOI maintains unparalleled depth and breadth of expertise across a range of oceanographic research areas. Institution scientists and engineers work collaboratively within and across six research departments to advance knowledge of the global ocean and its fundamental importance to other planetary systems. At the same time, they also train future generations of ocean scientists and address problems that have a direct impact in efforts to understand and manage critical marine resources.
http://www.whoi.edu/main/ocean-science-exhibit-center http://www.whoi.edu/who-we-are/ http://www.whoi.edu/who-we-are/

Comment: The author and the publisher assume that the informations in this book are correct at the time of publication. Please inform us if you wish to update and/or supplement the information. This will be taken into account if the book is reprinted.

Wikipedia, and further media had been consulted and used many times while writing this book.

Cover (Photos: See Fig. 11, Fig. 17, Fig. 3, Fig. 39, Fig. 7)
Inner Flap (Photo: Moshe Richards)
Contents (Photo: http://www.newmediareader.com/book_samples/nmr-21-nelson.
Fig. 0 (Photo: http://www.newmediareader.com/book_samples/nmr-21-nelson.
Fig. 1 (Photo: Wikimedia Commons.)
Fig. 2 (Photo: ©Jürgen Claus)
Fig. 3 (Photo: ©Jürgen Claus)
Fig. 4 (Photo: Wikimedia Commons.)
Fig. 5 (Photo: ©Jürgen Claus)
Fig. 6 (Wikimedia Commons)
Fig. 7 (Photo: ©Jürgen Claus)
Fig. 8 (Photo: Karl-Heinz Hochhaus, Creative Commons)
Fig. 9 (Photo: ©Jürgen Claus)
Fig. 10 (Photo: ©Jürgen Claus)
Fig. 11 (Photo: Archive submarin. magazin der unterwasserwelt.)
Fig. 12–14 (Photos: ©Jürgen Claus)
Fig. 15–18 (Photos: ©Jürgen Claus)
Fig. 19 (Photo: ©Submerged Resources Center)
Fig. 20 (Photo: Jacques Rougerie)
Fig. 21 (Photo: ©Archive Jürgen Claus)
Fig. 22 (Photo: Jürgen Claus)
Fig. 22 (Photo: Jürgen Claus)
Fig. 23 (Photo archive Jacques Rougerie)
Fig. 24 (Photo: Creative Commons)
Fig. 25 (Photo: Five Deeps Expedition)
Fig. 26 (Photo: ©Jürgen Claus)
Fig. 27 (Photo: Jürgen Claus)
Fig. 28 (Photo: ©Jürgen Claus)
Fig. 29 (Photo: Altaeros Energies)
Fig. 30 (Underwater Photo: ©Jürgen Claus.)
Fig. 31 (Photo: ©Nora Claus)
Fig. 32 (Photo: ©Jürgen Claus)
Fig. 33 (Photo: ©Jürgen Claus)
Fig. 34 (Underwater Photo: ©Jürgen Claus)
Fig. 35 (Photo: Andre Foulon)
Fig. 36 (Underwater Photo: ©Jürgen Claus.)
Fig. 37 (Photo: ©Jürgen Claus)
Fig. 38 (Photo: ©Jun Nguyen-Hatsushiba)
Fig. 39 (Photo: ©Jürgen Claus)
Fig. 40 (Photo: William Katavolos, Organics. Booklet published in 1961 by Steendrukkerij de Jong & Co., Hilversum. In this booklet, the text also appeared in a Dutch, French and German translation.)

Imprint

Concept and Text	Jürgen Claus
Graphic Design	2xGoldstein (Andrew und Jeff Goldstein, Erik Schöfer, Joshua Kaiss)
Copy editing	Marianne Grati-Kehrhaus
Printing and Binding	Dr. Cantz'sche Druckerei Medien GmbH, Esslingen

Distribution and marketing edition cantz
sales@edition-cantz.de

ISBN 978-3-947563-97-5

Printed in Germany

Published by edition cantz
www.edition-cantz.de

edition cantz

zentrum für kunst und medien karlsruhe